VICTORIAN
Dolls' House Projects
A DAY IN THE LIFE

VICTORIAN
Dolls' House Projects
A DAY IN THE LIFE

CHRISTIANE BERRIDGE

First published 2006 by
**Guild of Master Craftsman
Publications Ltd**
166 High Street, Lewes
East Sussex, BN7 1XU

ISBN 1-86108-463-3
ISBN 978-1-86108-463-7

This book is dedicated to my children,
Edward, Eleanor and Toby Berridge,
with much love.
Christiane Berridge

A catalogue record of this book is available
from the British Library.

Managing Editor: Gerrie Purcell
Managing Art Editor: Gilda Pacitti
Production Manager: Hilary MacCallum
Photography: Anthony Bailey
Editor: Clare Miller
Designer: Erica Smith

Typefaces: Garamond, Gill Sans and
Kuenstler Script
Colour origination by Wyndeham Graphics
Printed and bound by Sino Publishing

Note:
Although care has been taken to ensure
that metric measurements are true and
accurate, they are only conversions from
imperial; they have been rounded up or
down to the nearest convenient equivalent
in cases where the imperial measurements
themselves are only approximate. When
following the projects, use either imperial
or metric measurements; do not mix units.

Contents

Foreword

I have always enjoyed making miniatures whatever their historical period, but it is the stuffed pomposity of Queen Victoria's reign that I love the most. When I got the chance to act the role of a Victorian housemaid in a school's educational programme I grabbed it. It provided me with hands-on work in a Victorian house and was the closest I ever came to being a real Victorian servant. The experience made me want to fill my own dolls' house with even more miniatures now that I'd seen and used the real items for themselves.

I expect that, like me, you will already have bought several pieces of furniture for your own Victorian house. Now you want to add your own personal touch by including home-made items too. This book will enable you to do just that, including both familiar and more unusual pieces to complement those that you already have.

The materials I've used are generally inexpensive so that you can spend your money on those items that you can't easily make – glass and silver in particular, as well as quality furniture. While the eye is always drawn to craftsman pieces in a miniature room, your own hand-made items sit well around them.

If you already have a supply of paper, mountboard, strip wood, fabrics, paint and glue you are ready to start. You don't need more than basic craft tools, though I've found that a mini drill is useful. You may also be adept enough to swap mountboard for ⅟₁₆in (2mm) thick sheet wood.

With memories of my own Victorian working life in mind I have presented my projects as though spending a day inside the Victorian house, from the early rising of the tweeny (the maid who assists both cook and housemaid) to the end of a busy dinner party at nightfall. I just hope that you enjoy making pieces for your Victorian dolls' house as much as I have for mine.

Christiane

Christiane Berridge

The Victorian Era

The Victorian era is comfortably familiar to most of us. We learnt about the Victorians at school and can recall family stories passed down through the generations from our great-great-grandparents. Many of us live in houses from the period and are familiar with elements of their architecture – stained glass, encaustic floor tiles, sash windows, four-panelled interior doors, dado and picture rails. The fabulously floral designs of the late-Victorian designer William Morris are still popular today, living on as notebooks and giftwrap as well as in their original purpose as wallpaper and fabrics.

The Victorian period continued beyond the 64 years of Queen Victoria's reign to encompass those of her son Edward VII, and the years up to the First World War. From 1841 to 1901 there was an explosion in technical ability that influenced all aspects of domestic life, bringing new houses, new colours, new fabrics, and new styles. Queen Victoria ruled over a quarter of the globe and this too influenced what came into her subjects' homes in terms of artefacts and ornaments. It is no wonder that the Victorian people, particularly the growing middle class, embraced all this and filled their houses to the brim with examples of 'Victoriana'.

It is this overcrowding of domestic interiors that is so appealing to the miniaturist. With rooms filled with all manner of furniture, bric-à-brac, objets d'art and tasselled drapes, there is no obvious point at which a house interior can be described as 'finished'. It is always possible to add 'just one more item', unlike a Georgian room where style and elegance is dependent upon a classical minimalism, Victorian clutter is embraced warmly like a favourite aunt. Newcomers to the dolls' house hobby, like children in a sweet shop, will find that the Victorian era satisfies that desire to buy everything!

Victorian houses vary in size from the unassuming mid-Victorian terrace (right), to the more imposing home of a wealthy family (middle), to the ostentatious architecture of some houses, such as the Queen's own Osborne House (far right).

The Victorian House

A Victorian house can vary in size from the humble one-up-one-down, representative of the terraces of the burgeoning industrial towns, to the large Gothic mansion or Queen Anne revival house. The larger the house the more ostentatious it will be, reflecting the finances and social standing of the family within. Whatever the size of the house the internal layout should follow some basic rules. Servants and family occupy separate areas of the house with the domestic staff in the basement and attic floors.

The family occupies the ground-floor rooms and above. These rooms show some variation in décor. Those on view to guests are the most richly decorated – the hallway, parlour and dining rooms for example, again reflecting one's social standing. These rooms have higher ceilings, richer plasterwork (cornices, ceiling roses) and grander fireplaces. Upstairs, rooms are plainer and made distinctly private in real Victorian houses by creating a multitude of corridors and passages in the larger houses. Children are confined to the upstairs, or attic nursery whenever possible.

With the Victorian period spanning seven decades it is generally divided into three sections: early, middle and late. And there will be slight differences in style within each of these divisions.

Early Victorian

This covers from 1837 and Queen Victoria's accession to the throne until about 1860. The interior décor of homes follows on from the Regency period.

It features the pale colour palette of that period, as well as still adhering to the popular Regency striped wallcoverings, with crimson and gold being favoured in the main reception room and green in the drawing room, bedrooms and library.

Mid Victorian

The decorating styles of 1860 until around 1880 are the 'typical Victorian', with a plethora of colour, ornate wallpapers, rich swags of fabric and that overstuffed look. Developing industrial processes bring an increase of dyes and reduced prices to mass-produced furnishing materials. Interior walls are subdivided by dado rails, cornice and picture rails to provide plenty of opportunity to mix colours and patterns. Encaustic tiles in earth colours are used.

Gothic influences result in rich reds, greens and gold being used in the home. Medieval patterns have a major effect on the exterior of the home with towers, multi-paned windows and decorative brickwork frequently giving the home a clerical feel. Flock wallpaper is at the height of its popularity.

Early Victorian

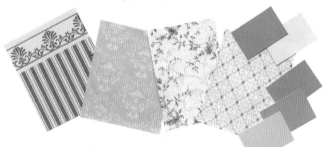

Mid Victorian

Late Victorian

Late Victorian

From around 1880 onwards the Arts and Crafts Movement began to influence a return to a softer palette for the domestic interior. Ochres, sage, plum and pale blues are favoured. Lighter woodwork is also chosen. So-called 'sanitary' wallpapers (washable) and heavily embossed borders and friezes become prominent again. Patterned tiles and those with motifs are used. Floorboards are stained or polished, parquet floors are an alternative, and removable carpets are popular as they can be taken out and easily cleaned. Interiors are becoming less cluttered.

In America the Victorian style exhibited itself in the terraced 'brownstone' houses and the colourful (and fanciful) 'painted ladies' with their verandas, balconies and gingerbread bargeboards. Furniture styles generally followed the English but made use of American wood.

Your Dolls' House

There is plenty of scope when selecting a dolls' house to suit your budget and the size and internal layout may dictate to some degree how you go about decorating it. You may decide to pinpoint a certain decade or you might even prefer a more general interpretation of the Victorian vision. The decision is yours – enjoy your dolls' house, don't worry about it!

When it comes to deciding exactly what to put in your Victorian dolls' house (or for any historical period) do some research. Become familiar with the period that you wish to copy by looking through books on the subject. There are plenty of titles available on full-size Victorian style; everything from architecture and interiors, to fashion and social life. This, or its nearest equivalent, is what you need to find but in miniature.

Take note of the patterns and colours used on wallpaper and fabrics, the style of furniture, the use of flooring materials and so on. Get a feeling for what house interiors really looked like by looking at guidebooks from stately homes and houses of this period.

What you include will also depend upon the size of your dolls' house and the number of rooms that you have to fill. Most of us want to include a kitchen, parlour and bedroom, but with more rooms at your disposal you could also have a dining room, a study, a nursery, and servants' bedrooms. Even larger still and your dolls' house could include a bathroom, a separate servants' hall, scullery, day and night nursery, library or dressing room! The choice is yours, and remember, by including false doors at the back of your dolls' house you can always suggest that further rooms exist.

Using your new-found knowledge it is much easier to identify suitable items when you are shopping for miniatures. Compile a scrapbook of favourite photocopied images or postcards of what it is that you are searching for. Take this with you to help identify what you need, and so spend wisely.

As soon as you start buying keep a record of what you buy and from whom. Keep hold of business cards and samples of papers to build up a reference guide to your own dolls' house. Small photograph albums are handy for this purpose. This is invaluable when it comes to dolls' house fairs and you wonder if a new furniture suite on show there might match your wallpaper. It also helps when you wish to return to a particular maker for further items. This guide is also beneficial if you wish to hand your dolls' house on to future generations, giving them not just a house, but its provenance too.

Construction Notes

Instead of being presented in the familiar room-by-room format, the dolls' house projects in this book are identified by the time of day at which they may be encountered. With obvious exceptions you can use the items in whichever rooms you wish. There is also an alphabetical index of projects at the back of the book to help you select what to make.

All of these projects should be easy to follow and present no problems. Most make use of tools and materials that you will already have such, as acrylic paints, brushes, cutting mat, steel rule, scissors, PVA and Tacky Glue. You will also need a selection of dolls' house wallpapers, fabrics and trimmings.

Most of the patterns are shown full size (ie: they are in 1:12 scale). Simply trace off the shapes to use as templates.

This section provides you with some useful hints for construction.

Using Mountboard

● Mountboard is a useful cardboard material. It is 1/16in (2mm) thick and is often used in my projects in place of wood. You can buy it from art and craft shops and may be also be able to buy a bag of inexpensive offcuts from picture framers.

● Mountboard comes in a range of colours, though often in the projects it is painted or covered over so colour is immaterial. However, you can make use of the colour – for example when lining boxes.

● Mountboard is best cut with a sharp scalpel or craft knife, and using a metal ruler and a cutting mat. Keep the blade upright to avoid cutting the board at an angle. It can be easily glued with PVA or Tacky Glue.

● When making a box the shorter sides are most often glued between the longer ones, before gluing all four sides to the base. Sometimes the base is made from thin card to help keep the scale better proportioned.

Gumstrip Sealing Tape

● Gumstrip sealing tape is a very useful commodity and can usually be bought from stationers' shops. It can help strengthen joints where mountboard pieces have been glued together. One side of the tape needs to be wetted for the glue to be activated. Do this with a paintbrush and jar of water to avoid the unpleasant taste of glue in the mouth, but apply the water sparingly.

● Once dry the paper is very strong and this benefits the construction of many miniatures. Left unpainted its buff colour resembles cardboard.

Thick Card

For many of the projects I have used thick card from an old set of alphabetical index cards. It is thicker than postcards, but not as thick as mountboard.

Veneer

● Items made from mountboard can be given the appearance of wood by covering with thin wood veneer. This is available from wood suppliers and some craft shops. I have found that Tacky Glue secures it firmly but wood glue also works well.

● Wood veneer should first be cut across the grain, then with the grain to minimize splitting.

● The easiest way of cutting the veneer to shape is to lay each surface to be covered face down on the veneer, then score around the perimeter with a sharp scalpel. The cut-out veneer can then be glued onto the item's surface. This method helps take account of any minor discrepancies in measuring. It works well on boxes.

● When covering a box veneer the two ends first, glue these in place, then measure and cut the longer sides. This means that the veneer will cover the ends of the previously applied veneer too as well as the underlying mountboard. With a box make sure the grain runs in the same direction.

● A fine sanding of the veneer before varnishing will improve the finish.

Wallpaper Paste

Brushing wallpaper paste onto cotton fabric and then draping or folding the fabric and leaving it to dry, will retain the shape of the fabric. This is very effective on bed sheets, shawls over chairs, and bath towels.

● Cover your base item in plastic food wrap first.

● Apply wallpaper paste on both sides of the fabric and shape it as desired.

● Leave to dry over a radiator until fully dry.

● Remove the plastic food wrap carefully and allow any inner areas to dry thoroughly too.

Early Morning

In the Maid's Bedroom

The first to wake in the Victorian household is the housemaid, whose day starts as early as 5am. Hers is a thankless job that involves all aspects of cleaning, with many chores to be done before breakfast is taken. Sharing a bedroom is inevitable.

With running water often available only in the basement, many a bucket is carried up and down the stairs. If the housekeeper and the family are fair the work being done is manageable, if tiring. With food and warmth available the job is attractive to many a country-born girl.

In the attic bedroom the maid hurriedly dresses and there is barely time to make the bed before racing down the back stairs to the servants' hall to begin her duties.

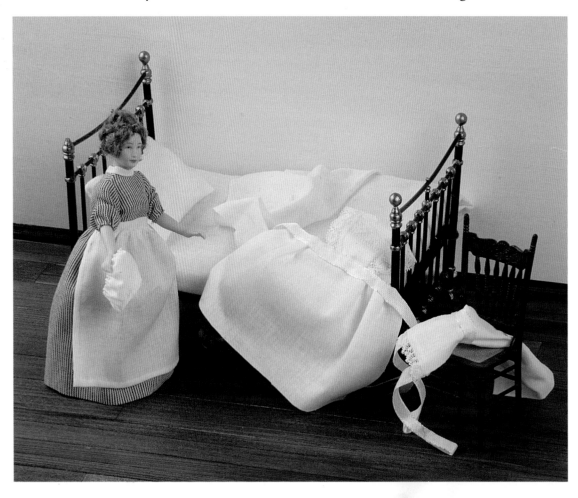

Maid's Apron

There are many styles of apron available to the domestic servant. Some have shoulder straps that link through the waistband to tie in a bow, others are fixed with pins to the bodice. Some households required their maids to have well-starched aprons so that their approach is heard by the family.

Materials
Strong white cotton fabric
White ribbon or cotton tape
Lace
Fray Check

For the plain apron

1 Cut the bib and skirt pieces using the templates. Fray Check the edges and leave to dry.

2 Decorate the top of the bib with narrow lace, gluing it to the reverse side.

3 Sew the bib to the skirt section.

4 Gather the waist to measure 3in (76mm).

5 Glue a length of ribbon or tape to make the apron ties.

6 Glue a length of ribbon or tape to make the shoulder straps. Fold a loop at the end of each strap for the waist ties to thread through.

Plain apron

PLAIN
BIB
Cut 1

APRON SKIRT
Cut 1

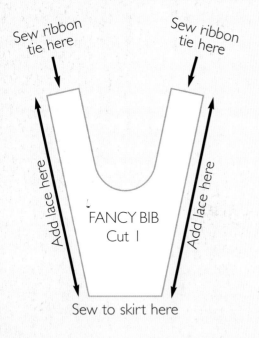

For the fancy apron

1 Cut out the bib and skirt section using the templates. Fray Check the edges and leave to dry.

2 Glue on apron ties as with the plain apron (page 13).

3 Decorate the front of the bib and the shoulder straps with fancy lace.

Fancy apron

Sew ribbon tie here

Sew ribbon tie here

Add lace here

Add lace here

FANCY BIB
Cut 1

Sew to skirt here

APRON SKIRT
Cut 1

Rumpled Bedding

Having rumpled bedding in the bedroom can really make your dolls' house seem lived in. It is a simple effect to achieve.

Materials
Cotton sheet (or fine handkerchief) to fit the bed
Wallpaper paste
Wide brush
Plastic mat
Plastic food wrap

1 Cover the bed and mattress with plastic food wrap to protect them.

2 Mix up a small quantity of wallpaper paste according to the manufacturer's instructions.

3 Lay your sheet on the plastic mat and cover liberally on both sides with wallpaper paste.

4 Take the sheet carefully to the bed. This is a messy procedure as the sheet will cling to itself because of the paste.

5 Tuck the end of the sheet at the foot of the bed and fold the top edge down.

6 Now fold back the sheet creating folds and wrinkles as in real life. Arrange these creases until you are happy with the finished effect.

7 Make sure that any part of the sheet that would touch the floor is folded to rest along it.

8 Leave the bed beside a radiator until completely dry (overnight is best).

9 Remove the sheet carefully – it should retain its moulded shape – and take away the plastic food wrap. Replace the sheet and put the bed back into the dolls' house.

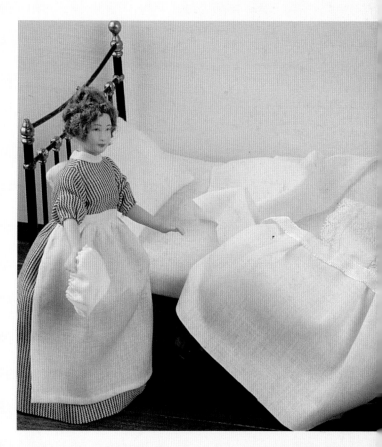

The maid's bedroom is sparsely furnished with a simple candle for light. Tallow candles are cheap but pungent. The housekeeper often sells the stubs of wax candles on to pedlars to re-form and resell.

Clothes are aired over a rack near the open fire.

Hidden away at the top of the house the servant rises early from a narrow bed often tucked away under the eaves.

In the Servants' Hall

The number of female servants is increasing, particularly in middle-class households. Books are now available on how to manage your servants including Mrs Beeton's *The Book of Household Management*, which is packed full of domestic advice. Any large household has a pecking order of servants, and each one aspires to advance up the ranks.

If your dolls' house is large enough use a basement room as the servants' hall where the domestic staff can gather to eat, as well as undertake a variety of their duties. Include a large table for eating and performing tasks, a couple of comfortable chairs for the senior domestic staff – the housekeeper and butler – and plain wooden chairs for the others, as well as dressers for storage.

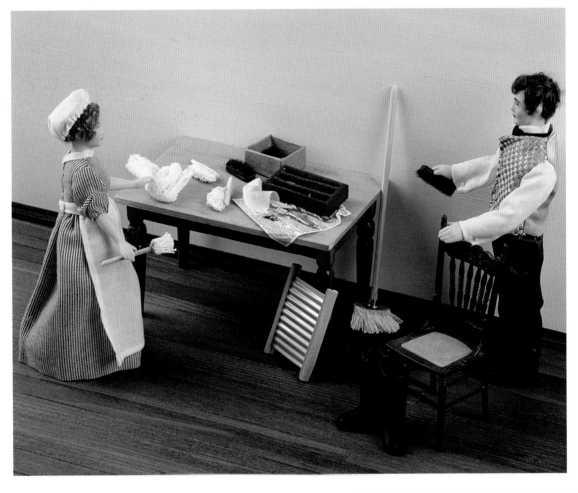

Girls from poor backgrounds will begin to look for work as a domestic servant from the ages of 12 or 13. Country-born girls are deemed easier to train up than city-born children. They will begin their training with very basic chores such as scrubbing or vegetable preparation. By the age of 21 a hard-working girl may hope to have become a housemaid and have less of the menial chores to undertake. By 30 she may look to be a lady's maid and another decade on, a housekeeper.

The housekeeper is the head of the female servants, and on a par with a butler in terms of status. She is referred to as 'Mrs' (whether married or not).

Her badge of office is the large bunch of keys that open the still room and the linen room (and the box of tea). Part of her role is making sure that the other female servants know theirs, particularly as regards discipline and cleanliness. She is responsible for the hiring and firing of other female staff except the nursery staff and the lady's maid.

Often the housekeeper will invite the other upper servants to her parlour to eat separately from the lower servants, maintaining the hierarchy that exists below stairs as well as above. She has seen that the maids are already about their duties.

Materials

White crochet cotton
PVA glue
Matchsticks
Wooden cocktail stick
Bamboo skewer
Jump ring
Thin card
Metal eyelet

Making the fringing

1 Cut a 12in (305mm) length of crochet cotton. Secure one end to your work desk with a mini clamp, or a piece of sticky tape. With the thread rising at an angle, secure the other end at another point higher up (this can be in the middle of the thread, and can be adjusted as you work the fringing). This makes the key thread.

2 Cut several 2in (51mm) lengths from the crochet cotton to form the fringing. It is easier to work with longer pieces for now than the finished size required.

3 Take a piece of the fringing thread and fold it in half to make a loop. Hold the loop behind the key thread, but bring the tails of the loop in front of the key thread then over it and through the looped end. Pull tight and this knots the fringing thread into place on the key thread.

4 Continue threading on loops of crochet cotton until you have a length of fringing to work with. Un-clamp the key thread.

5 Trim the length of the fringing after it has been made to the required size.

Fringing for brushes

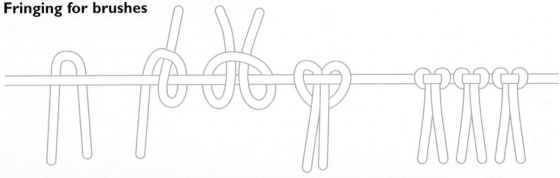

Hand-held Brush

1 Make a 2in (51mm) length of fringing.

2 Fold the fringe in half and then half again and compress between your fingers.

3 Open out the length slightly and apply PVA glue carefully along the edge of the fringing and fold up again. Press tightly or clamp until dry. This forms the bristles.

4 Cut a matchstick to 1in (25mm) and using a craft knife or scalpel, carefully shape the end, rounding with a little sandpaper if necessary.

5 Glue the matchstick handle to the fringe bristles and leave to dry.

Stiff Bristled Brush

1 Make a length of fringing then coat it in PVA glue and leave to dry before continuing with the construction.

2 When dry tease out the bristles carefully with the point of a compass to stop them looking too clumped.

Washing-up Brush

1 Make a short length of fringing as before and wrap around the end of a shortened cocktail stick using glue to secure.

2 When the fringing is dry add a little glue to the top and slip on a small jump ring.

Soft Head Broom

1 Make a head of bristles as for the hand-held brushes using a 3–3½in (76–89mm) length of fringing. Fold and glue the bristles to form the broom head.

2 Glue this to a thin shaped piece of card.

3 When dry glue an eyelet to the end of a 4in (102mm) length of bamboo skewer (add a collar of paper to ensure a snug fit). Glue this to the centre of the broom head.

Like the housemaids the footmen are also early risers, getting up around 6am. The family has left their boots and shoes outside their bedroom doors to be cleaned and polished. In larger households these are collected and taken to 'the boot room' to be dealt with, otherwise the job is done in the servants' hall.

Shoe Shine Brush

Materials
Six pieces of mountboard ¾ x ¼in
(19 x 6mm)
Self-adhesive Velcro (only the loop/fluffy side is used)
PVA glue
Flexible sanding block
Brown acrylic paint

---

1 Glue two pieces of mountboard together three times. Leave for glue to set. These become three brush backs.

2 Shape the ends of each back by holding the mountboard between the finger and thumb and rubbing the sanding block against it in a curving motion.

3 Paint the sides and brush back in brown acrylic paint. Leave to dry.

4 Glue a piece of loop fastener to each back, trim around to match the shape of the back.

5 Varnish the brush back and sides.

Brush Box

Make a cardboard box to display the boot brushes (perhaps for a shop window).

Materials
1 piece of cardboard ¹³⁄₁₆ x ¾in
(20.5 x 19mm)
4 pieces of cardboard ¾in x ⅜in
(19 x 10mm)
PVA glue
Gumstrip sealing tape

---

1 Glue the sides to the base of the box.

2 Strengthen the construction by covering in gumstrip sealing tape.

Brush box

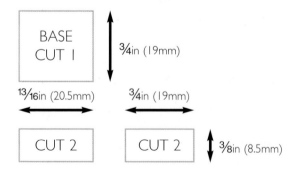

Wash board

In large households the laundry is sent away to be cleaned, having been carefully recorded in the housekeeper's accounts, and dispatched in large wicker baskets. Soap is applied to soiled areas of a garment, such as necks and cuffs, and rubbed on the washboard before being put into a tub to soak.

Materials
Aluminium drinks can
Tacky Glue
Strip wood with grooves
Corrugated paper maker
Strong scissors or tin snips

1 Slightly crush the can and cut into the fold using the scissors. Cut out the body of the tin to form a rectangle.

2 From the tin cut a section 2¼ × 1½in (57 × 39mm).

3 Carefully fold this section of tin in half with the printed side of the can on the inside. Use the edge of a metal ruler to help achieve a flat edge.

4 Put the tin section through the corrugated paper maker.

5 Cut a 1¾in (45mm) section from the wood strip.

6 Cut lengthways down the wood strip to leave two pieces with a central groove.

7 Using a scalpel pare away down the length of the wood to make the shape more rounded.

8 Apply Tacky Glue down each long side of the corrugated tin section and push between the grooved strip, one for each side. Leave to dry.

The eradication of dust is a relentless chore for the housemaids. A wide variety of brushes is needed. There are banister brushes, hearth brushes, shoe brushes, bottle brushes, crumb brushes, dusting brushes, carpet whisks and feather dusters, as well as the basic scrubbing brush. The maid carries the brushes and other cleaning cloths in a wooden box from room to room.

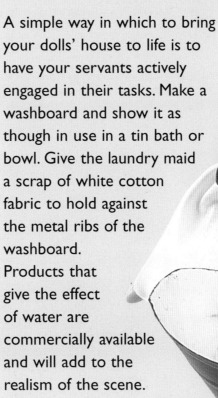

A simple way in which to bring your dolls' house to life is to have your servants actively engaged in their tasks. Make a washboard and show it as though in use in a tin bath or bowl. Give the laundry maid a scrap of white cotton fabric to hold against the metal ribs of the washboard. Products that give the effect of water are commercially available and will add to the realism of the scene.

In the Master Bedroom

The master and mistress do not rise early, unlike the servants. Their four-poster bed is now considered unfashionable as the drapes are believed to harbour unhealthy germs. A replacement iron bedstead has been ordered to bring their bedroom up to date.

The Victorian fashion is to match linens, co-ordinating the curtains with the bedcovers. Heavier fabrics are used in the winter, and lighter ones in the summer. The wooden floorboards in the bedroom are regularly scrubbed and rugs removed and beaten.

The Four-poster Bed

Measure your bedroom ceiling height carefully and adjust the post height if necessary. This bed is quite narrow so that it can be accommodated in a smaller bedroom.

Materials
Four 8in (205mm) veranda posts
⅛in (3mm) square woodstrip
Dolls' house skirting board
⅛ x ½in (3 x 12mm) woodstrip
Lolly sticks
Mountboard
Acrylic paint
Varnish
Silk fabric
Iron-on interfacing

1 Cut the veranda posts carefully to leave a 2½in (63mm) plain section at the bottom.

2 Cut a slot 1in (25mm) up from the bottom of each post, long enough to fit the ½in (12mm) wide woodstrip that will form the side and end rails of the bed. The slots need to be ⅛in (3mm) deep. By inserting the rails into the corner posts the construction is a little stronger than just using butt joins, although you may prefer to do this. You need to make the slots of two adjacent sides of each post.

3 Cut two lengths of ⅛ x ½in (3 x 12mm) woodstrip to form the side rails. These need to be 6¼in (159mm) long to fit into the slots (or 6in (152mm) if making butt joins). Cut two lengths of ⅛ x ½in (3 x 12mm) woodstrip to form the end rails. These need to be 4¾in (120mm) long to fit into the slots (or 4½in (114mm) if making butt joins).

4 Glue the rails into the slots, supporting the assembly carefully and making sure that it is square.

5 Cut the ⅛in (3mm) square woodstrip into two lengths of 6in (152mm), and two lengths of 4½in (114mm). Glue these to the lower edge of each side and end rail to form a ledge to take the mattress supports later.

6 The skirting board needs to be cut to form the top rail. You need two pieces that are 6in (152mm) plus double the width of your veranda posts, and two pieces that are 4½in (114mm) plus double the width of your veranda posts. Mitre the ends carefully.

7 Glue the top rails in place, ⅛in (3mm) proud of the top of the corner posts. Leave to dry, making sure that the assembly is square.

8 Measure and cut enough lolly sticks to form the slats that will support the mattress across the width of the bed base. Leave a small gap between each slat. You will find it easier to space them equally if you start with one slat across the middle and then position the rest.

9 Cut a piece of mountboard, 6in × 4½in (152 × 114mm) to form a ceiling – check the fit and amend if necessary. If you want a curtain to hang at the head end of the bed, cut the ceiling mountboard a little shorter in length to accommodate the curtain, which can be glued to the head end of mountboard and taken down to the floor.

10 Put the mountboard to one side while you paint the bed frame with acrylic paint in shades of brown. Varnish when the paint is dry.

11 While the varnish is drying cut a piece of silk fabric, 7in × 5½in (178 × 140mm) and cover one side of the mountboard 'ceiling', pulling the silk taut, and gluing to the reverse. Carefully trim the corners to reduce the bulk.

12 Cut a piece of interfacing, 6in × 4½in (152 × 114mm), position centrally onto a piece of silk fabric, 7in × 5½in (178 × 140mm), and iron to secure.

13 Carefully iron the edges of the silk over the interfacing to form a neat rectangle. Glue this to the reverse of the silk-covered piece of mountboard.

14 Put the ceiling into position, resting it on top of the four corner posts.

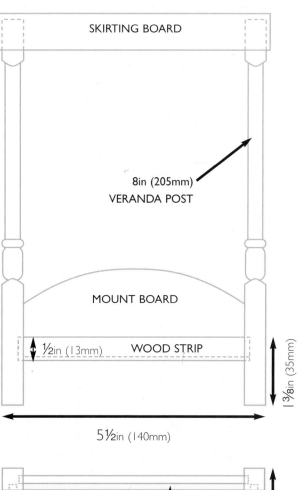

SKIRTING BOARD

8in (205mm)
VERANDA POST

MOUNT BOARD

½in (13mm) WOOD STRIP

1⅜in (35mm)

5½in (140mm)

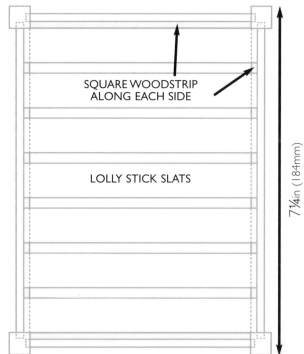

SQUARE WOODSTRIP
ALONG EACH SIDE

LOLLY STICK SLATS

7¼in (184mm)

Corset

Many of the undergarments that enable the Victorian lady to display a fashionable figure are uncomfortable. The corset exaggerates the bust and hips, and by drawing in the waist, makes its narrowness all the more obvious.

Materials

Cream or white cotton fabric – look for a fabric that has a striped pattern to resemble whalebone shaping.
Iron-on interfacing
Fray Check
Lace and braid
Crochet cotton or embroidery thread
Tacky Glue
Double-eyelet picot braid

1　Cut a rectangle of fabric 3¼in × 2in (82 × 50mm), and back with interfacing.

2　Cut out the corset shape using the template, and Fray Check all the edges.

3　Sew the darts as indicated.

4　Fold over the back edges ³⁄₁₆in (5mm).

5　Glue looped braid down each back edge.

6　Thread up a needle with crochet cotton or four strands of embroidery thread.

7　Leaving a 2in (50mm) long 'tail' sew from the bottom to the top, then back down again, forming a criss-cross pattern of lacing. Leave another tail before cutting the thread.

8　Drag the tails through a small dab of glue and wipe between your fingers. When the glue dries the 'tails' will stiffen slightly, binding the embroidery threads together.

Corset

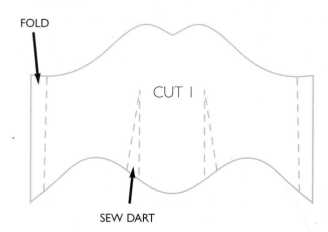

FOLD

CUT 1

SEW DART

Washstand

The Victorians often paint their pine furniture with a faux-paint effect to resemble a more expensive wood, such as mahogany.

Materials

Four staircase spindles, 2½in (63mm) long (legs)
Piece of wood ⅛in (3mm) thick and 1⅝in x 2½in (41 x 63mm) (top)
Piece of wood ⅛in (3mm) or less, and 2⅛in x 1⁵⁄₁₆in (54 x 33mm) (lower shelf)
Two lolly sticks, cut to 3in (76mm) retaining curve at one end
Two lolly sticks, cut to 1⅜in (35mm)
Wooden cocktail stick
Marble effect Fablon
Ceramic jug and bowl

Washstand

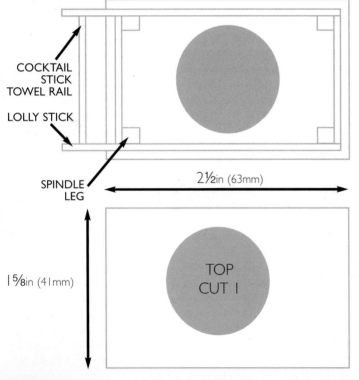

COCKTAIL STICK TOWEL RAIL

LOLLY STICK

SPINDLE LEG

2½in (63mm)

1⅝in (41mm)

TOP CUT 1

1 Measure the diameter of your bowl and mark out a circle in the centre of the table-top just a fraction smaller than the diameter of your bowl.

2 Carefully cut the circle and lightly sand the inner edge then cover the table top, and sides with Fablon, cutting away the central hole.

3 Put the round-ended lolly sticks together and drill a hole ¼in (6mm) away from the curved end, big enough to take the cocktail stick.

4 With the table-top face down, glue the lolly sticks ¹⁄₁₆in (2mm) in from the edges of the table top to create the sides then glue a staircase spindle into each corner to provide legs.

5 When the glue has dried carefully insert a length of cocktail stick to provide a towel rail. Sand the ends of the stick flush with the sides for a neat finish.

6 Cut a shaped lower shelf from the wood, measuring carefully in between the table legs for a close fit.

7 Gently indent the corners with a piece of sandpaper wrapped around a cocktail stick to fit against the legs.

8 Glue the shelf to rest on the shaped band on the legs and paint the wood or varnish if you prefer.

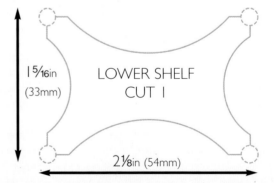

1⁵⁄₁₆in (33mm)

LOWER SHELF CUT 1

2⅛in (54mm)

Mourning Jewellery

Strict rules govern the period of mourning in Victorian times. Jet jewellery is popular, with Whitby in Yorkshire being a prime source of the material.

Materials

Self-adhesive black beads
Black rocaille beads
Thin white card
Thick black paper
Varnish
Cream self-adhesive dolls' house carpet
Gold acrylic paint
Acetate
Tacky Glue

1 Cut a ¾in (19mm) square of card and cover with a piece of dolls' house carpet.

2 Place the black beads on the card in the shape of a necklace. When happy with the arrangement, glue into place. Leave for the glue to dry.

3 Paint a small gold dot at the back of the necklace to represent a clasp fastening.

4 Use the template to cut out the necklace box from black paper.

5 Carefully fold the sides and glue to make up the box. Varnish when dry to strengthen.

To make a 'loose' necklace cut a 'V' shape from a piece of acetate and glue the beads onto this. Alternatively, cut out an oval shape from acetate and glue the beads to the outside of this. This shape can be placed (or secured with Blu Tack) on the top of a dressing table or chest of drawers. The same techniques can be used with coloured beads to make a range of jewellery for evening and day wear.

Jewel case

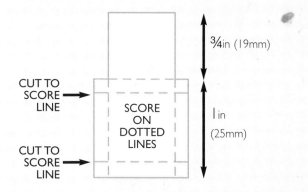

¾in (19mm)

CUT TO
SCORE
LINE →

SCORE
ON
DOTTED
LINES

1in
(25mm)

CUT TO
SCORE
LINE →

A whole trade has developed around the mourning of loved ones. Jet jewellery is popular and available in a wide variety of pieces from rings and bracelets to ornate necklaces.

The fashionable figures that women are expected to display require the wearing of corsets beneath their elegant gowns. Unfortunately corsets can distort young growing bodies and produce a variety of digestive and reproductive problems.

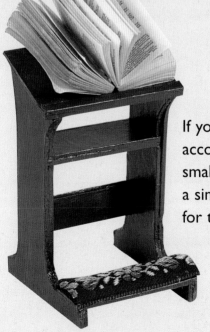

If your dolls' house can accommodate it, create a small family chapel. Otherwise a simple prie-dieu will suffice for those daily prayers.

In the Nursery

The baby of the household is in the care of the head nurse, with the older children in the charges of the nursemaid. From cleaning and feeding, to dressing and entertaining, their domain is the top floor of the house. This is far away from the adult lives led below but also where the air is believed to circulate more freely and away from the smells of the kitchen. In large households there is a day nursery for play and education and a separate night nursery for sleeping. The day nursery is light and airy with the upper sash of the window frequently left ajar to let in a healthy breeze.

With a length of stiff wire and some wide ornate lace you can transform a purchased cot into a canopied delight for your dolls' house nursery. Add coloured bows to suit the little ones or use white or cream for a nostalgic theme.

Fancy Cot

Materials
Ready-made cot
Foam – ½in (13mm) thickness
Cardboard
Striped fabric
12in (305mm) thin but sturdy wire
2in (51mm) wide lace
Narrow ribbon

1 Cut a piece of foam to fit the base of the cot (or add another piece to the existing mattress) to create a new mattress that is ½in (13mm) thick.

2 Glue a piece of card to the base of the foam and cover with striped fabric, gluing over the foam and to the card to secure.

3 Drill a hole centrally in the head and footboards of the cot and correspondingly below at the base level.

4 Take a piece of wire and bend into a curve.

5 Place each end through the holes made in the cot ends and into the base hole. Adjust the length of wire if necessary. Remove the wire.

6 Cut two strips of lace the length of the wire, Fray Check the cut ends if wished.

7 Place the strips of lace beside each other and overlapping slightly down the length.

8 Thread the wire through both pieces of lace along the length that stands proud of the cot. Thread the lace-free wire ends back into position in the cot.

9 Gather and tie the central piece of lace with a short piece of ribbon.

10 Lightly glue the ends of the lace to the ends of the cot.

Lace-ruffled Cover

Materials
Cotton fabric
Narrow lace
Sewing thread
Narrow ribbon

1 Cut a paper template to the finished size of your cover. The width should be that of the mattress. Position the template on a piece of cotton fabric and cut with a ½in (13mm) margin all around.

2 Mark the corners of the paper template with pins. Sew a continuous length of lace starting with the outside edge and working towards the centre of the cover. Overlap each row slightly. Finish off by sewing a ribbon bow in the centre.

3 Carefully pin the outside run of lace towards the centre.

4 Cut a second piece of fabric to form the other side of the cover. With right sides facing, sew around three sides, take care not to catch the pinned lace.

5 Turn the cover the right way out, removing the pins as early as you can.

6 Sew up the remaining side.

Lace-ruffled cover

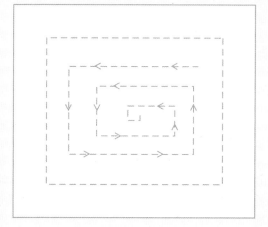

Picture Blocks

With a little patience picture blocks are easy to make. The choice of pictures is important, with sentimental scenes of children or animals making a suitable decoration.

The blocks shown here make use of Kate Greenaway's pictures of children found in an inexpensive book in a charity shop.

The scale of the images chosen is also important. Pictures where the detail is small is more in keeping, but it can be difficult to assemble the blocks in the right order. Larger images are easier to 'play' with but are really oversized in 1:12 scale. I've made use of both types to show you the contrast.

Materials

12 square wooden beads, each ¼in (6mm) along each side
Thin card
Mountboard
Gumstrip sealing tape
Suitable images
Black felt-tip pen

Set of blocks

1 Line up your square beads so that there are three rows of four beads and draw around them onto a rectangle of card. Cut out this area leaving a small border, like a picture frame.

2 Use this frame to help you select six images for your picture blocks. Using a sharp pencil draw around the inside edge of the frame on your chosen image and cut it out.

3 Carefully mark the image into 12 squares, each one the same size as a face of one of your beads. Cut these individual squares out.

4 Apply a small amount of glue to one face of one of the beads and carefully apply one of the squares of the image. Don't worry about holes in the beads as these will be covered with paper. You may find a pair of tweezers is helpful.

5 Put this block to one side and repeat with the second bead, and another square of image. Repeat until all 12 beads have one face covered.

6 Repeat the process working through all six images. Each time put the beads aside to make sure that you don't put two squares from one picture on one bead.

Making a 'matchbox'-style box

1 This is the simplest type of box – it works just like a matchbox.

2 Cut out a template from card to make the base. Cut out the corner squares and score the marked lines.

3 Fold up the box and use strips of gumstrip sealing tape to seal the corners. Use more tape to cover the base of the box.

4 Cut another strip of card as marked, Check against your box before scoring the fold lines. You are looking for a snug fit and you may find that you need to adjust the template slightly.

5 Glue the overlap edge and cover the outside with gumstrip sealing tape.

6 Glue a spare picture on the lid of the box to indicate the contents.

7 Use black felt-tip pen to cover the exposed cut edges of the box if you wish.

Making a box with a lift-off lid

1 Make a box base to contain the beads as before but make it a little taller.

2 Enclose this box with strips of mountboard ¹³⁄₁₆in (22mm) wide, leaving the top of the card proud like a collar.

3 Make a lid for the box using a card base that is the same size as the box base. Use more strips of ¹³⁄₁₆in (22mm) mountboard to make four sides. Glue these strips to the lid and cover with gumstrip sealing tape to strengthen.

4 The lid should fit snugly over the card collar of the base of the box.

5 Glue a picture on the lid.

'Matchbox' style box

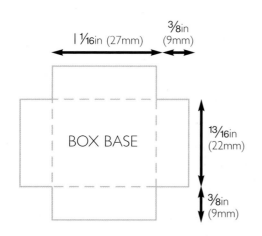

BOX BASE

1 ¹⁄₁₆in (27mm) ³⁄₈in (9mm)

¹³⁄₁₆in (22mm)

³⁄₈in (9mm)

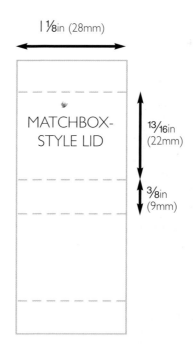

1 ¹⁄₈in (28mm)

MATCHBOX-STYLE LID

¹³⁄₁₆in (22mm)

³⁄₈in (9mm)

Children under nine years old are expected to have a midday sleep in a darkened room. A baby can be put into the cot or cradle for his nap. The nursery is at the top of the house so that children are neither seen nor heard by the rest of the household. They are under the charge of the nursemaid and bought to the drawing room to see their parents between teatime and dinner. Larger households will have a day and a night nursery.

Away in the nursery the children are playing quietly. Toys are generally instructive and educational rather than frivolous and fun. Picture blocks are easy to make, if a little time-consuming. For realism get your child to hold a block and pile up some of the others so that the scene looks less static.

Mid-Morning

In the Kitchen

Mid-morning finds the kitchen a hive of activity. Hidden from public view, and often partly below ground-level in the basement, the resulting poor light and ventilation creates a hot and stuffy working environment. The room has a flag-stoned or tiled floor and whitewashed walls (though blue is also believed to keep flies at bay). A large cast-iron range dominates the room. A dresser provides ample storage and is often built-in like a piece of fitted furniture today. A large scrubbed table is central to many tasks. If your dolls' house is large enough you could house the glazed stoneware sink and plate rack in a separate scullery, otherwise create a corner for them in your kitchen.

Kitchen Table

Materials
Piece of wood 5½ x 3½in (140 x 89mm)
for the table top
Four square newel posts (legs)
Bamboo skewer
Woodstrip

1 Sand each corner of the table top to provide a gentle curve.

2 Cut the newel posts so that each measures 2½in (63mm). Cut carefully to provide shaped 'bun' feet if possible.

3 Using the diagrams as a guide, drill holes to accommodate the utensil rack, and the side hanging rail in the legs.

4 Cut lengths of woodstrip to fit in between the legs, and glue to the underside of the table top.

5 Prepare the bottom utensil rack by cutting lengths of woodstrip the width of the table top and gluing them across two lengths of bamboo skewer.

6 Cut a length of bamboo skewer to fit between the two legs at one end of the table to form the hanging rail.

7 Carefully glue the legs into position, accommodating both the utensil rack and the hanging rail. Hold until the glue takes making sure that the table is square.

8 Paint the table as appropriate.

Table (50% of actual size)

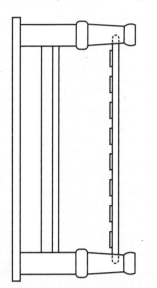

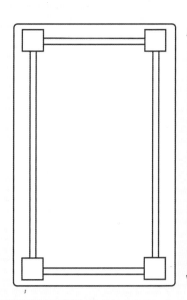

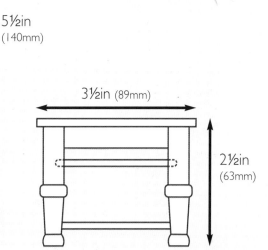

5½in (140mm)

3½in (89mm)

2½in (63mm)

Sugar Cone

Sugar is delivered in large cones, and pieces are 'nibbled' off using tongs when required.

Materials
White Fimo
Bamboo skewer
Tacky Glue
Caster sugar
Paper plate

1 Make a cone shape of white Fimo, approximately 1¼in (32mm) tall with a ⅝in (16mm) base. Shape the top as though a chunk of sugar has been 'nibbled' off.

2 Make a hole in the bottom of the cone, approximately ½in (13mm) deep.

3 Bake according to manufacturer's instructions.

4 When cold insert a length of bamboo skewer into the hole at the base.

5 Holding the piece of skewer cover the cone in glue, and sprinkle generously with caster sugar. Prop the skewer and cone upright for the glue to dry.

6 When the glue has dried, remove the skewer and glue the cone onto a plate.

Copper Flan Dishes

Materials
Copper-coloured card
Mountboard
Tacky Glue
Corrugated card maker
Copper enamel paint
Polyfilla (optional)
Cream acrylic paint (optional)

1 Cut out strips of card of various widths, from ¼in (6mm) to ¾in (19mm).

2 Roll the strips through the corrugated card maker to 'crinkle' them.

3 Form each strip into a circle with the copper colour on the outside. The diameter isn't crucial, and can vary between 1 and ½in (25 and 13mm).

4 Place each circle on a piece of mountboard and draw around the interior, twice.

5 Cut out these two circles smoothing out the corrugated 'bumps'.

6 Glue the circles together add a smear of glue to the bottom of the corrugated circle on the inside. Push the mount-board into the circle to form the base.

7 When dry paint the base and the inside with copper enamel paint.

Cake Mixture

Mix up a small quantity of Polyfilla adding a little cream acrylic paint. Put a dollop of the mixture into the flan dish, swirl with a cocktail stick and leave to dry.

Cheeses

Cheeses are easy to make using cork, which resembles the crumbly nature of some cheeses. Use pictures of real cheeses as a guide to colouring.

Materials
Cork from a wine bottle
Yellow, green, blue and white acrylic paint

1 Cut a cork into three slices, each measuring about ½in (13mm). Each slice will make one cheese. You can cut them narrower if wished.

2 Cut 'slices' out of some of the cheeses.

3 Paint the cheeses with acrylic paint as appropriate.

Tips on painting

Paint a base coat of one colour onto the cork, and then use other colours sparingly to blend on top. Dab the colours on with a fine paintbrush. Smudging with your fingertips helps to blend the colours.

Use the end of a square-tipped paintbrush to add 'blue veins'.

You can always re-paint the cheese if you are unhappy with the finished result.

If you can't paint simply cover a cylinder of cheese with cotton tape as if it is wrapped in linen.

Bread

Materials
Cork from a wine bottle
Brown and cream acrylic paint

1 Cut a ¾in (19mm) section from a cork.

2 Shape the cork by cutting or sanding.

3 Carefully sand the edges with fine sandpaper to smooth, and round the end of the loaf.

4 Paint the crusts, and any cut surfaces. Paint any 'buttered' side in a suitable yellow.

Ornate jellies and desserts are a feature of elaborate dinner parties. The larger estates have ice-houses in their grounds to store cold foodstuffs. Ice creams, mousses and sorbets could be presented fashioned in ornate moulds. Raspberry, peach and strawberry are popular flavours.

Vermin had to be got rid of! Rats and mice such as these make a realistic addition to the dolls' house kitchen or attic, unlike their full-size examples, which are never welcome!

Household deliveries, including bread, are made at the back door of the domestic quarters. Look for a bicycle with a large wicker basket to park outside the back door.

In the Hallway

The hallway of a Victorian house must make a good impression on guests. It often includes imposing furnishings alongside practical ones. A dado of anaglypta paper covers the bottom portion of the wall, as shown, and is frequently varnished to protect it from the inevitable knocks and scrapes. A hall table should be included as a place for callers to leave their visiting cards.

Stuffed Bear

Hunting exotic game in India or Africa for the Victorian gentleman is considered a pleasure. The master of this house is no exception and he has displayed his trophies where visitors can admire them. Animal skin rugs frequently grace the floors of hallways, studies and parlours, glass-eyed antelope heads stare out from the walls, and an elephant's foot might provide a receptacle for walking sticks and umbrellas.

Look for plastic animals in toy or gift shops that can be adapted for the dolls' house. The animal can be made more realistic by adding 'fur.' Standing the animal on a plinth also gives it a little more height to suggest the correct scale.

Materials

Plastic bear
Dolls' hair (wigging material)
White, black and pink acrylic paint
Varnish
PVA glue
Block of balsa wood
Wood veneer
Wood glue

To add a 'fur' coat

1 Paint the bear's eyes and mouth with acrylic paint to give them better definition. Add a tiny drop of varnish to the bear's eyes to suggest glass eyes. Leave to dry.

2 Select lengths of dolls' hair in brown and black, and, over a saucer, snip into tiny pieces. You may wish to make a pile of black and a pile of brown with a further pile of a mix of the two.

3 Working from the ankles of the bear, cover approximately 1in (25mm) of one leg with PVA glue using a paintbrush to take account of any textured surface that your plastic animal may have.

4 Pinching a small amount of fur between your finger and thumb, drop this over the glued area. Dab it gently with your fingertips to help it stick.

5 Work your way over the entire surface of the bear aiming to finish with the head. You may wish to add more definition to certain areas (such as the belly) by just using the black. The colour difference should be subtle.

6 Work the area around the facial features carefully. Clear any hairs around the eyes, nostrils and mouth with a cocktail stick.

7 Turn the bear around to check if you have missed any areas – although 'bald' patches will create an authentic aged look. Leave the glue to dry thoroughly.

Making the plinth

1 Decide on the size of base that your bear needs to stand on.

2 Cut your base from a block of balsa.

3 Edge each side of the block in turn with wood veneer. Keep the woodgrain running in the same direction around the sides. Clamp while the glue dries.

4 Gently sand the wood veneer and then varnish it.

5 Stand your bear on top, glued in position for security.

6 Add a brass plaque showing the date of 'capture.'

Zebra Skin

Materials
White felt 7 x 5in (178 x 127mm)
Beige felt 7 x 5in (178 x 127mm)
Black embroidery thread
Black acrylic paint
Thick paper or thin card

1 Cut out the zebra skin shape from the piece of white felt.

2 Cut out a second zebra shape from the beige felt, but this time cut it slightly larger around the legs, tail and 'waist'.

3 Mark out the stripes on a piece of thick paper or thin card. Cut these away with a scalpel to create a stencil.

4 Place the stencil over the white piece of felt. Dip a brush into the black paint, being careful not to overload it.

5 Stipple the brush over the stencil to create the black stripes.

6 When completed carefully lift the stencil away and leave the felt to dry. If you have missed any of the stripes, or want a stronger colour, repeat the painting process.

7 Make a 1¼in (32mm) length of fringing from the black embroidery thread (using the same method as for the brushes on page 20) for the mane and tail hair. Keep a length of thread at each end of the fringed section.

Zebra skin

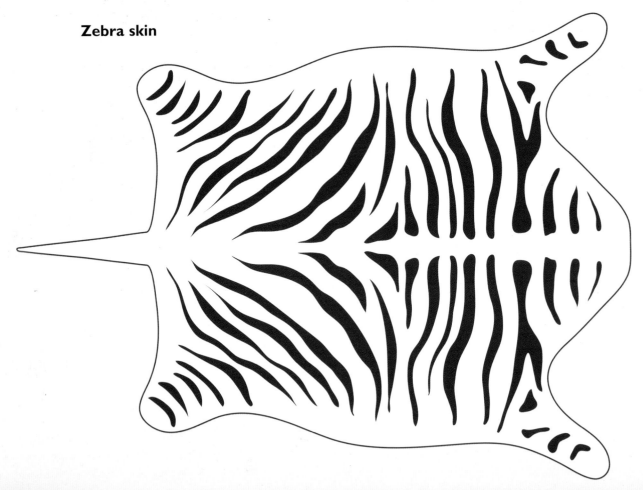

8　Either glue the fringed mane in place or sew it in position as follows. Thread a needle on one end of the loose threads and insert it about 1¼in (32mm) in from the 'head' of the skin, pull it through to the underside of the skin until the fringing is against the felt. Re-thread the needle on the other end of the loose thread and insert it just in from the 'head' end, again pulling the fringed thread taut against the felt. This time use three or four stitches to catch the length of fringing securely against the felt. Knot the thread off on the underside of the white felt.

9　Glue the white piece of felt to the beige piece securing another length of fringing of just three 'knots' between the two pieces of felt at the tail end.

10　Trim the mane hair so that it is shorter at the neck end and curves towards the head, and brush to one side using a pin to unravel the individual strands of thread.

Materials

Toilet roll tube
Mountboard
Thin card
Gumstrip sealing tape
Black felt tip pen
Dolls' house wallpaper
Imitation 'scaled skin' fabric
PVA glue
4 jump rings

1　Cut a 1⅛in (29mm) section and a ⁵⁄₁₆in (7mm) section off the toilet roll tube.

2　Cut two circles of mountboard, 1⅝in (42mm) diameter.

3　Push the mountboard circle to the bottom of the larger section of toilet roll tube – it should be a snug fit. This forms the box.

4　Cut a piece of Gumstrip ½in (13mm) wide to go around the base of the tube. Turn the tube base side up and stick the Gumstrip with ¼in (6mm) proud of the base. Slit this 'proud' piece and fold to enclose the base.

5　Cover the outside of the tube with a couple of layers of Gumstrip to strengthen it.

6　Line the inside bottom of the box with a piece of dolls' house wallpaper.

7 Colour the rim of box (and lid) with black felt-tip pen.

8 Push the second mountboard circle into the smaller section of toilet roll tube to form the lid. Cover with Gumstrip as previously, and line with dolls' house wallpaper when dry.

9 Cut a 1¼ x 5in (32 x 127mm) strip of thin card. Pull between your finger and thumb to curl it.

10 Fit the card strip inside the box to check the size. There should be no overlap just a butt join. Glue the card strip in place to form the box collar.

11 Cut a 2in square of 'skin' fabric and with the skin side down, glue the base of the box to it. When dry cut around the box. Repeat with the lid.

12 Cut a strip of fabric skin to go around the sides of the box and the lid. Glue into place. Make sure that the join in the fabric matches the join of the card collar on the box section.

13 Cut a strip of fabric skin to go across the lid and down both sides of the box. Shape the strip in the middle and taper the ends. Glue onto the top and sides of the lid.

14 Cut two shorter pieces of fabric skin to glue to the sides of the box, slipping two jump rings onto each strip before gluing into place. Glue one of the strips across the join of fabric to hide it.

Carpet Bag

Black watery paint will add a suitable patina of age to the fabric on this bag.

Materials
3¼in (83mm) length of 2in (51mm) wide dolls' house stair carpet
Black cotton tape
Black leather
Fray Check
4 gold jump rings
Tacky Glue
Balsa wood
Brass pins

1 Cut out two ends from the balsa wood using the template. Carefully round the edges with sandpaper. Cover with black leather, gluing it in place and pulling it taut. Leave to dry.

2 Fray Check the ends of the stair carpet. When dry enclose (and glue) the ends of the stair carpet with a 2in (25mm) wide length of black cotton tape.

3 Glue the stair carpet around the balsa ends. Push brass pins into the ends of the carpet to resemble studs.

4 Cut two thin strips of leather, 1½in (39mm) long, and two lengths of 1in (25mm) to form the straps.

5 Thread two jump rings onto each of the shorter straps then thread the longer straps through them before gluing in position on the bag.

6 Cut two handles from the leather and glue into position.

7 Squash the bag by pushing the ends to give a little character.

CUT 2 FROM BALSA

SPINDLE

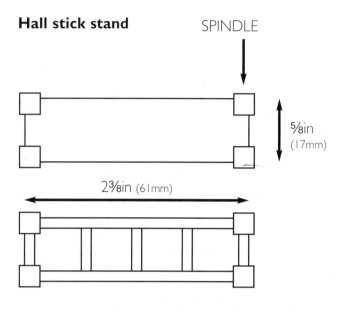

⅝in (17mm)

2⅜in (61mm)

Hall Stick Stand

This slim stand for holding walking sticks and umbrellas works perfectly in the narrow hallway.

Materials

Four square-based spindles
Jumbo lolly stick (try craft shops) or piece of wood
⅛in (3mm) square woodstrip
Wood glue
Shades of brown acrylic paint
Varnish

1   Cut the jumbo lolly stick (or piece of wood) into a rectangle to form the base cutting a square from each corner where the spindles go.

2   Cut the woodstrip into two lengths of 2⅛in (54mm), and two lengths of ⅜in (9mm).

3   Glue two short and two long pieces of the cut woodstrip onto the lolly stick to form an edge rail.

4   Cut two more lengths of woodstrip, 1⅛in (28mm), and three pieces of woodstrip ⅜in (9mm) long. Use these to make a 'ladder', gluing the shorter pieces between the longer ones. Leave to dry.

5   Glue the spindles into the corners of the base, leaving about ⅛in (3mm) proud to form the feet.

6   Carefully glue the ladder piece between the sets of legs, ¼in (6mm) from the top. Cut two more ⅜in (9mm) lengths of woodstrip and glue between the legs at the shorter sides.

7   Check that the assembly is square and leave to dry completely.

8   Paint in shades of brown and varnish when dry.

Putting luggage in the dolls' house hallway suggests that the occupants have either just come back from a trip or are about to go on one. It therefore provides the hint of a story for the viewer to imagine.

The Victorians had no qualms about stuffing and mounting their hunting spoils. Hunting trophies are easy to make given the wide variety of plastic animals available. Here, the head has been removed from a plastic goat and covered with 'fur' before being mounted on a wooden shield.

Adapt the instructions for this zebra skin to try another animal pelt, such as a leopard or tiger. Sometimes you can find fur fabric that will also work in miniature to produce a realistic looking skin. Long fur can always be trimmed shorter. Remember that bright white fabric can usually be died with tea or coffee to make it look older, experiment on a piece of scrap fabric first.

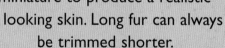

In the Master Bedroom

With the family occupied elsewhere in the house the chimney sweep (arriving by the tradesmen's entrance) sets about his duties. Despite the grimy nature of the work, he must be sure to leave no mess.

Chimney Sweep's Brush

The chimney sweep's rods screw together to form enough length to clean the flue.

Materials
Black crochet cotton
PVA glue
Wooden dowel ⅛in (3mm) diameter
or bamboo skewer
Black eyelet
Brass-coloured paper

1 Make a 4½in (114mm) length of fringing using the same method as for the brushes (page 20).

2 Place the fringing on a piece of plastic (an old mat or bag) and liberally coat in PVA glue. Leave to dry thoroughly.

3 Using the point of a compass carefully separate those strands of the fringe that have formed into clumps.

4 Cut the dowel into several 3in (76mm) lengths and paint black to form the rods. It doesn't matter how many you have – enough to suggest a length to be pushed up a chimney!

5 Coat one side of the fringe along the knotted edge with glue

6 Holding a rod perpendicular to your worksurface wind the fringe around the end of the rod several times, pressing the glued edge down on itself to form the brush head. Leave to dry.

7 Push a black eyelet down onto the brush head.

8 Add a small band of brass-coloured paper to suggest the screw joins, standing proud of the dowel.

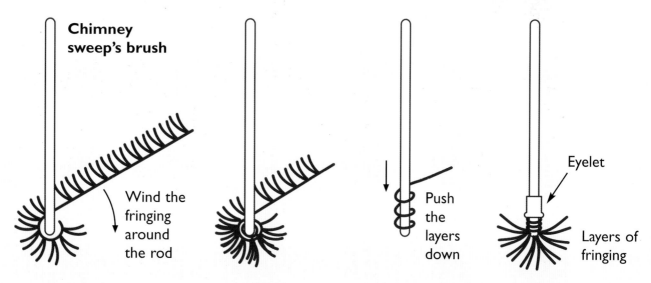

Chimney sweep's brush

Wind the fringing around the rod

Push the layers down

Eyelet

Layers of fringing

Coal Box

Materials
Mountboard (black on one side or paint black)
1in (25mm) length of black cotton tape
PVA glue
Wood glue
Small brass drawer knob
Satin varnish

1 Cut out the pieces from the mountboard, remembering to reverse one of the slanted side pieces so that the black surfaces will be facing the inside when the box is made.

2 Using a fine sanding block carefully slope the top edge of the front piece so that it matches up with the sides.

3 Glue the sides to the base and back, then the front to the sides and base. All the black surfaces should face inwards.

4 Using a fine sanding block carefully slope the top edge of the top piece to match up with the slant of the sides. Glue into place.

5 Using a fine sanding block carefully slope the front and back edges of the lid piece. Hold the lid against the box with your fingers to check the shape of the slope.

6 Glue the cotton tape onto the top of the box. If the tape is wide align it with the back of the box.

7 Holding the lid in position glue the rest of the tape to the lid. There should be a slight gap between the top and the lid pieces to allow the fabric to act as a hinge and not impede the movement of the lid.

Coal Box

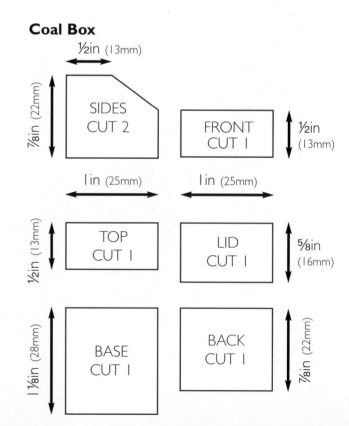

To cover the coal box

1 Cover one side with wood veneer.

2 Repeat for the other side making sure that the wood grain is running in the same direction.

3 Using wood glue stick the veneer pieces to the sides of the coal box and clamp until dry.

4 Repeat for the other surfaces of the coal box, continuing with the back, then the front, the top and the lid. You do not need to veneer the base. The veneer can split easily so take your time, or keep the split pieces and glue them in sections onto the relevant sides of the box. Clamp until dry.

5 Gently sand all sides and edges using a fine sanding block. Wipe away any dust.

6 Use satin varnish on all surfaces except the base and leave to dry.

7 Finally, add a small brass knob to the lid, and fill the box with chunks of 'coal'.

Note: The contents of this coal box have been produced by crushing up a piece of real coal. Put a piece of coal into a polythene bag and place on the floor. Crush the contents using a wooden rolling pin and then distribute where needed. If you don't have coal to hand, cut up irregular pieces of balsa wood, paint them black and use these instead. You can also suggest that the embers are still glowing. If you have a miniature general store you can make sacks of coal out of hessian with the tops open to show the contents.

A strict hierarchy of servants exists in larger Victorian houses under the watchful eye of the housekeeper. Even poorer households will generally boast one maid-of-all-work.

Until bathrooms become commonplace washing is done at a marble-topped washstand. The hot water is brought up from the basement kitchen or scullery to whichever bedroom requires it. After ablutions the dirty water has to be removed.

Without central heating a fireplace is essential in every room. More ornate ones exist in the family's rooms and plainer ones in servants' quarters. Many dolls' houses come with chimney breasts but they are also easy to make from balsa wood or mountboard. Measure the floor to ceiling height and match the cornice and skirting board so that they become part of the room.

Midday

In the Parlour

With the family occupied in the drawing room the housemaid continues her cleaning routine in the parlour. With so many ornaments to dust and surfaces to clean there is plenty to do.

As the day wears on an unseen army of servants makes their way through the family's rooms cleaning them thoroughly.

Each servant has his or her own responsibilities in the pecking order of the domestic hierarchy. Positions of trust are given to those who have earned them.

The housemaid is hoping one day to become a housekeeper so that she can earn more money and enjoy having a bedroom to herself. Though she may have to move to another household to do so.

Antimacassars

Our Victorian gentleman is fond of using macassar oil to give a shine to his hair, but it leaves its mark on upholstered furniture. A solution is to use pieces of cloth across the backs of the chairs. These are laundered on a regular basis.

Materials
Fine cotton fabric
Narrow lace
Fray Check
Tacky Glue

1 Cut as many antimacassars from the fine cotton fabric as you need for your chairs. If you have a sofa remember to cut enough to cover the back.

2 Apply Fray Check around the edges of the antimacassars and leave to dry.

3 Apply a thin line of Tacky Glue all around the edges of the antimacassar.

4 Take the lace around the edges of your antimacassar, allowing it to curve slightly around the corners and end with a slight overlap. Glue the lace into position. Take care to make tiny crimps as you glue the lace around any curves. Leave to dry.

5 Position the antimacassar on the chair.

CUT AS MANY
AS REQUIRED

Fringed Shawl

Shawls and throws are useful to disguise cheaper furniture. Paisley is a popular pattern originating in India.

Materials
Silk tie with Paisley pattern
Three colours of embroidery thread
Fray Check
PVA glue
Mini clamps

1 Unpick the tie seams and remove any backing. Iron the fabric carefully.

2 Cut a piece of silk, approximately 4in (102mm) square. Fray Check the edges.

3 Create a length of fringing (see page 20) choosing your own order of colours. Blue, green and bronze are used here.

4 Repeat the sequence of colours until you have a fringe long enough to go all around your silk material.

5 Apply a thin line of glue around the edges of the silk. Carefully glue the fringe to the edge tying the ends of the key thread in a knot and trimming neatly.

6 Once the fringing is dry trim to a ⅜in (9mm) length.

7 Carefully pull a pin through the fringing to untwist the individual strands of thread.

Baby Sculpture

Our family has already lost two children in infancy, which is not unusual in the Victorian age. Marble casts have been made of their limbs – a sentiment that seems mawkish to our modern minds – and are displayed on velvet cushions about the home.

Materials
White Fimo
Red fabric
Small piece of mountboard

Note: It is important to keep your hands clean when making these pieces so as not to discolour the white Fimo. The idea is to make a forearm and fist, so if you are familiar with doll-making this will come easily to you. If you can't make a limb use part of a doll kit instead to provide the arm, just paint it white.

1 Take a piece of white Fimo and roll it into a sausage shape about ½in (13mm) long, and ³⁄₁₆in (5mm) in diameter (the smaller the better).

2 Make a paddle shape at one end of the sausage with a narrower band below it to represent the wrist.

3 Cut five 'fingers' into the paddle and carefully shape, cutting the thumb shorter than the rest. Curl the fingers over, smoothing any cracks.

4 Bake according to manufacturer's instructions.

5 Glue to a piece of mountboard covered in red fabric.

Stereoscopic Viewer

A stereoscopic viewer creates the illusion of depth in a two-dimensional image, by presenting a slightly different image to each eye. First invented by Sir Charles Wheatstone in 1838 it provides an interesting diversion.

Materials
Mountboard
Thick card
1 matchstick
Tacky Glue
Burnt sienna & burnt umber acrylic paint
Satin varnish
Fancy wooden fan
Dome stickers (or acetate)
Small black and white images

1 Cut out the mountboard using the templates.

2 Cut a section from the fancy fan and glue to the rectangle of card.

3 Cut the matchstick into two ¾in (19mm) lengths.

4 Glue the two frames together, then glue these to the base section. Leave to dry.

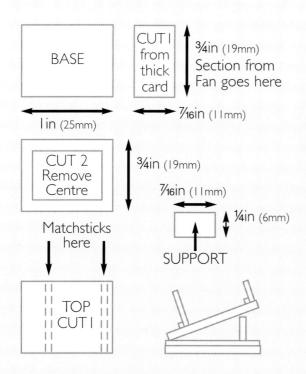

BASE

CUT 1 from thick card

¾in (19mm) Section from Fan goes here

1in (25mm)

7⁄16in (11mm)

CUT 2 Remove Centre

¾in (19mm)

7⁄16in (11mm)

Matchsticks here

¼in (6mm)

SUPPORT

TOP CUT 1

Waxed Flower Dome

Some miniatures arrive under plastic domes. Use these domes to resemble glass display cases.

Materials

Plastic dome and base
Selection of small flowers
Tacky Glue
Small piece of polystyrene
Brown & black acrylic paint
Varnish

Stereoscopic viewer

5 Cut two holes using a hole punch from another piece of mountboard to form the eyeholes. When you are happy with the spacing (it may take you several attempts) cut around the holes so that they are central to a rectangle, ¾in (19mm) by ⅜in (9mm).

6 Paint all the pieces with a mix of burnt sienna and burnt umber acrylic paint and leave to dry.

7 Carefully punch out two circles of plastic from the dome stickers or acetate and push these into the eyeholes.

8 Glue the assembly together as indicated in the diagram and varnish when dry.

9 Make viewing images by duplicating a picture and gluing them in pairs onto a small rectangle of card to stand against the fancy piece.

1 Trim a piece of polystyrene into a cone shape with a flat base to fit inside your dome (here ¾in (19mm) diameter by 1½in (39mm) tall).

2 Place the polystyrene cone on a piece of card, then generously cover the cone with Tacky Glue.

3 Cutting the flower stems shorter where necessary, glue the flowers to the cone. Flowers with a shortened wire stem can be pushed into the polystyrene to help secure them. Use smaller buds towards the top. Leave to dry.

4 Mix up a watery solution of black and brown acrylic paint and brush over the flowers to tone down any bright colours. Leave to dry.

5 Carefully brush on varnish to the various blooms and leave to dry.

6 Glue the flowered cone to the plastic base and replace the dome cover.

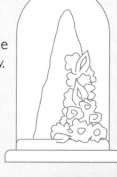

The ladies of the house and their visitors wear a variety of lovely gowns. Make use of silk and natural material if you are dressing your own dolls, as these fabrics are easier to work with than synthetics. Use patterned fabric with caution and ensure that any patterns are in a suitable small scale.

Sir Edwin Landseer is one of Queen Victoria's favourite painters. He appeals to the Victorians' love of sentimentality by endowing animals with the appearance of human emotions. Pictures of animals, particularly those that may be hunted, such as this noble stag, are a suitable choice for the study or dining room.

A bust of the monarch is a must-have in any Victorian house. Reigning for such a long period of time, and heading a large family and empire, Queen Victoria is a revered figure.

In the Scullery

Where laundry is done at home, Wednesday is the day for mangling and ironing. Laundry without pleats, such as sheets and table linen, is put through the mangle. Items that are pleated need a careful hand by the laundry maid with one of the smaller hand irons or the crimping mangle. The work is hard and has to be finished by the time that afternoon tea is to be served. Before laundry is finally put away the mending has to be seen to with any repairs carefully executed.

Table-top Ironing Board

Materials
Thin white cotton fabric (can be
'yellowed' in places)
Balsa wood
¹⁄₁₆in (2mm) wooden sheeting
Tacky Glue
White felt

1   Cut out the pieces using the templates.

2   Glue the two support pieces to the
base and leave to dry then glue the
white felt to the top and leave to dry.

3   Cut a piece of white cotton fabric on
the bias. Glue to the felt top of the
ironing board, pulling the cotton taut.
You might find this easier to do by
holding the piece in your hands and
crimping the edges over. Apply a little
extra glue to any overlaps as required.
Leave to dry.

4   Glue the padded board to the support.

BASE
CUT 1 FROM WOOD

Iron

Materials
Mountboard
Thin wire
Black leather
Tacky Glue

1   Using the template, cut out three iron
shapes from mountboard.

2   Glue the three pieces together, and
leave to dry.

3   Carefully shape the iron with fine
sandpaper then paint black and leave
to dry.

4   Pierce two holes in the top of the iron
without going through to its base.

5   Roll a thin rectangle of leather around
the middle of a 1½in (39mm) length
of wire.

6   Folding the wire into a handle shape
and trimming as necessary, insert the
two ends into the holes to form the
handle. When sure of the fit, remove,
coat the ends of the wire with glue and
re-insert.

Iron and ironing board

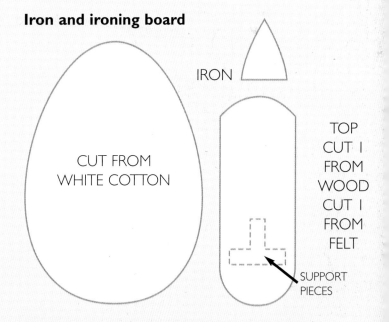

IRON

CUT FROM
WHITE COTTON

TOP
CUT 1
FROM
WOOD
CUT 1
FROM
FELT

SUPPORT
PIECES

Iron Heating Stove

In larger households a separate ironing stove makes it possible to heat up several flat irons at the same time.

Materials
Mountboard
Gumstrip sealing tape
½in (13mm) wooden dowel
⅛in (3mm) square woodstrip
Dolls' house banister moulding
Black spray paint
Pin
Earring 'butterfly'
Ring (optional)

1 Cut the dowel to match the height of your laundry room or scullery. Here it is 9in (229mm).

2 Cut a length of mountboard, 3½ x 6in (89 x 152mm).

Iron heating stove

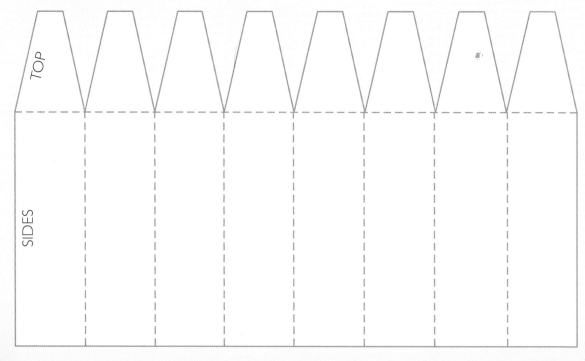

3 Score the mountboard into eight sections, each ¾in (19mm) wide. Score another line widthways 1in (25mm) from the top across all the section.

4 Cut the top sections according to the diagram.

5 Carefully fold the shape into an octagon. Glue the shape together leaving a hole for the dowel in the centre.

6 Cover the structure with gumstrip sealing tape.

7 Cut the top plate 1¼in square (32mm) with a hole for the dowel chimney.

8 Use a compass point or old ballpoint pen to score narrow lines across.

9 Push the dowel chimney into place and push the top plate down into position.

10 Glue short lengths of square strip wood to form the iron retainers just above the angled line.

11 Cut through the banister to form an 'L' shape and glue a second set of lengths, 1½in (39mm) from the base of the stove. These are quite fragile so handle them carefully.

12 Cut an arched stove door and glue to one segment at the base, use the pin and 'butterfly' to form a handle.

13 Spray the whole assembly black. Spray several thin layers rather than one thick one for the best effect.

14 Thread the ring above the iron plate to finish off.

Bloomers

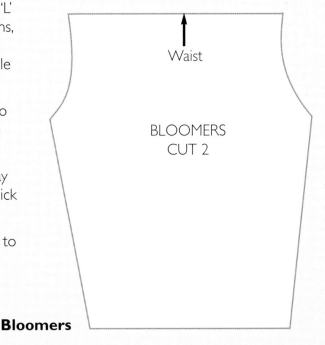

Materials
Fine white cotton
8in (205mm) narrow lace
Fray Check
Needle and thread

1 Cut out two legs from white cotton fabric using the template.

2 Fray Check the waist and lower edges of the legs and glue a double row of lace to each leg.

3 Folding the leg in half with the lace on the inside, sew each inside leg seam. Repeat for the second leg.

4 Use tweezers to turn one of the legs the right way out. Insert this leg inside the other so that the right side of each leg is touching. Sew up the crotch seam and turn the bloomers right side out.

5 Turn over a small hem around the waist, pull up slightly to gather and tie off. Place on the ironing board.

Waist

BLOOMERS
CUT 2

Irons come in a variety of sizes in the Victorian household. From larger box irons to small crimping and goffering irons. Fashionable pleating requires specialist equipment to keep it presentable.

Unless the household has sufficient servants to cope, washing is sent out to a laundry to be cleaned. These often employ 'fallen women' or single mothers in an attempt to reform their characters through hard manual work.

Servants are generally hired for a year. Offences for dismissal included immoral behaviour, being drunk, theft and disobedience.

In the Second Bedroom

The mistress's sister is preparing to travel by ship to India to join her fiancé. Being accompanied by one's maid is essential on visits away from home and discretion is vital. As an upper servant the lady's maid has her own bedroom and is much envied by the lower ranks for this privilege. Even so, a lady's maid is not allowed to retire to bed until her mistress has done so, as a maid's help is required with the complicated process of undressing.

Cape

Queen Victoria popularized tartan fabric following her purchase of the Scottish Balmoral estate in 1852.

Materials
Main fabric
Lining fabric
Hook and eye to secure
Matching sewing thread

1 Cut out the cape shape using the template from both pieces of fabric.

2 With right sides together sew around the outside of the pieces leaving a small turning gap in the middle of the hem.

3 Turn the cape right side out and sew up the gap.

4 Carefully fold and press as indicated to form a collar and two front turnings.

5 Stitch the hook and eye as indicated to form the fastener.

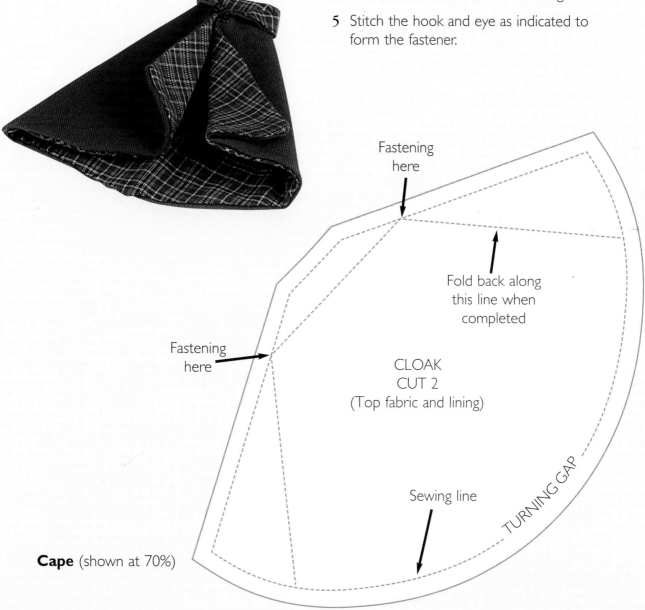

Fastening here

Fold back along this line when completed

Fastening here

CLOAK
CUT 2
(Top fabric and lining)

Sewing line

TURNING GAP

Cape (shown at 70%)

Travelling Trunk

Chests of drawers made out of matchboxes can still have a place in the dolls' house, if you use them carefully. This travelling trunk has five drawers but you could make more or fewer as required.

Materials

3 matchboxes
Mountboard
Thin card
Gumstrip sealing tape
Dolls' house wallpaper
Beading wire
7 silver beads
Black felt-tip pen
Black cotton tape

Making the drawers

1 Remove the contents of the matchboxes.

2 Remove the drawer from one of the matchboxes. Measure ¾in (19mm) from the end of the drawer and cut. Keep the remainder.

3 Use the thin card to make a new end for the drawer.

4 Glue the new end in position and use gumstrip sealing tape to strengthen. Cover the new shorter drawer with a single layer of gumstrip sealing tape making sure that it still fits snugly into the outer case. Leave to dry.

5 Place the drawer on top of the case, mark the depth and cut accordingly.

6 Repeat the process to make five drawers. One matchbox should provide two drawers.

Enclosing the drawers

1 Glue the stack of five casings on top of each other. The structure will seem unstable so use gumstrip sealing tape around the outside to strengthen it.

2 Measure the sides of the stack of drawers and cut two pieces from the mountboard to match. Glue these to the sides and clamp them in place while the glue dries.

3 Cut two pieces of mountboard to form the top and the bottom. Glue these in position and clamp while the glue dries.

4 Cut a piece of mountboard to cover the back. Glue in place and use Gumstrip to strengthen the joins at the top and bottom.

5 Colour any cut edges black using the felt-tip pen.

Making the other sides of the trunk

1 From the mountboard cut two sides, a top and base and a piece for the back to make a matching half (although this can be narrower than the drawer section).

2 Glue the long sides between the top and base. Glue on the back. Use gumstrip sealing tape to strengthen all joins.

3 Colour all the exposed edges using the black felt-tip pen.

4 Cover the interior with wallpaper.

5 Using a compass point make two holes in the top, central to the front and back.

6 Bend a piece of wire to form a hanging rail and push through the holes, gluing a silver bead on the inside top where the wire goes through the hole.

7 Bend the excess wire to lie flat against the top and cover with a piece of gumstrip sealing tape.

Finishing off

1 Cover each drawer front with a piece of dolls' house wallpaper.

2 Make a hole in the centre of each drawer with a compass point.

3 Thread a bead onto a 1in (25mm) length of beading wire then thread the wires through the hole, leaving the bead as a drawer knob.

4 Fold back the wires on the inside of each drawer to lie flat against the drawer. Cover the inside of the drawer front with a piece of gumstrip sealing tape to hide the wires.

5 Place the two sides of the trunk together, open sides facing. Glue a 3in (76mm) length of cotton tape to form a spine. Leave to dry.

6 Cover with Aida fabric, paint and add leather bindings.

Buy or make other pieces of luggage such as this trunk. It contains a removable tray for smaller personal items.

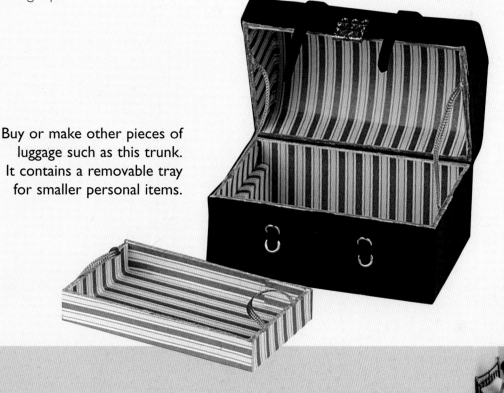

Fancy hats need to be looked after carefully and stored in special boxes. They are easy to make, requiring little more than ribbon or bows to decorate. They are also inexpensive to buy in towering sets of diminishing sizes.

Hunting is not just an idle pastime, it also supplies the fashion trade and the table. Fur stoles such as this one are favoured.

A hard-working housemaid would hope to make her way up the servant hierarchy. A good reference is essential to move between households.

In the Study

In his study the master of the house writes a number of letters of business. The room is a masculine preserve and decorated accordingly in sombre colours.

The postal service was introduced shortly after Queen Victoria came to the throne. It is a vital means of communication for business and personal matters. Like many other Victorian activities letter writing is governed by etiquette. Young ladies, for example, cannot write to a gentleman unless he is a relative or her fiancé.

Also kept in the letter rack are calling cards. Etiquette rules that calls are to be made between three and six in the afternoon, with no formal call lasting longer than 15 minutes. They should have been announced by a card being left – a lady would leave her own card, plus two of her husband's.

Letter Rack

Materials
Mountboard
Thick card
Tacky Glue
Fancy wooden fan
(optional)
Burnt umber and
Burnt sienna
acrylic paint

1 Cut out all pieces using the templates.

2 Cut a piece of wooden fan to fit the front piece to provide decorative detail.

3 Paint all in a mixture of burnt sienna and burnt umber acrylic paint.

4 Cut narrow strips of mountboard to help divide the main sections. These don't need to be painted.

5 Glue the sections into place, beginning with the back piece placed on the base, then add a narrow strip before adding the next.

6 When all the pieces are in place glue the two sides into position.

BACK

SIDE
CUT 2

MIDDLE

LOWER
BASE

MIDDLE

BASE

FRONT

Letter rack

Blotter

Materials:
1⅜ x 1⅛in (35 x 28mm) piece of card
(1/32in (1mm) thick)
1⅜ x 1⅛in (35 x 28mm) piece of quality writing paper
Small scraps of leather
Black felt-tip pen

1 Colour the cut edges of the card with a black felt-tip pen.

2 Cut a ½in (13mm) square from the leather, cut diagonally in half, then cut these two pieces in half again to give four triangles.

3 Glue the paper to the card and leave to dry.

4 Glue a leather triangle at each corner of the blotter, pressing each firmly.

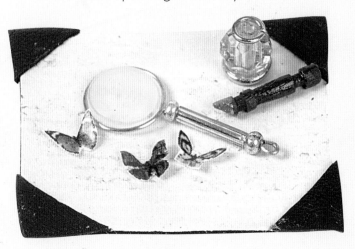

Inkwell and Pen

Materials
Glass bead
Gold jump ring
Fancy-ended cocktail stick
Tacky Glue
Black and gold acrylic paint
Varnish

1 Glue the jump ring to the blotter, then glue the glass bead on top to make the inkwell.

2 Cut a ½in (13mm) section from the fancy end of the cocktail stick. If you don't have one of these you can use a plain one, or find a fine fancy dowel.

3 Trim one end into a nib shape using a scalpel.

4 Paint the body of the pen black and the nib gold. Leave to dry.

5 Glue to the blotter then, using a fine paintbrush, apply a thin layer of varnish to the pen.

Magnifying Glass

The magnifying glass is stuck to the desk blotter so that it doesn't get lost. This also makes it easier to construct.

Materials
⁵⁄₁₆in (8mm) diameter self-adhesive clear plastic protective pad
2in (51mm) thin (bead) wire
2 small gold beads
1 gold tube bead (⁵⁄₁₆in (8mm) long)
Tacky Glue
Paper butterflies (optional)

1 Wrap the wire around the protective pad to form a loop. Cut off any excess on one end of the wire.

2 Bend the other end of the wire at 90° to the loop to form a 'circle on a line' shape.

3 Thread on one gold bead, the tube bead, then the second gold bead.

4 Cut off the end of the wire to leave a very small piece that can be bent using pliers to form a small loop, which stops the beads falling off.

5 Stick the protective pad into position on the desk blotter. Dab a small amount of Tacky Glue on the back of the handle and, positioning the wire loop over the protective pad, glue to the blotter.

6 Carefully glue three butterflies on the desk blotter as specimens to be examined. Those used here came from a photocopied birthday card.

Oriental Fan

The Great Exhibition of the Works of Industry of all Nations in 1851 (and subsequent displays) bought to the Victorian householder an idea of what other countries could produce. Japanese art and design was particularly admired, and by 1870 quite a craze had developed in Britain for the Japanese style.
It might be said that oriental geometric forms and natural motifs were to be superseded by a home-grown variation under the direction of William Morris.

Consider making an oriental room in your dolls' house, or perhaps a lacquered display cabinet. Inexpensive plastic 'Chinese' folding screens can often be bought from dolls' house shops and fairs. Look for carved beads that could pass for ivory ornaments.

Materials
Mountboard
Beading wire
Tracing paper
PVA glue
Embroidery thread
Small bead
Tube beads
Black acrylic paint (optional)

1 Use the template and cut out a fan shape from cardboard.

2 Wrap a length of wire around the cardboard fan, and overlap one end around the other at the neck of the fan.

3 Cut away the excess on one side. Remove the cardboard.

4 Apply glue sparingly around the wire 'circle'.

5 Tying a knot of embroidery thread around the wire at the neck wind embroidery thread around the wire 'circle', finish off with another tight knot.

6 Thread your beads onto the handle of the fan, which measures approximately ¾in (19mm).

7 Cut the wire close to the end of the beads, leaving just enough to bend into a small loop. Before closing the loop completely, tie a piece of embroidery thread to form a tassel.

8 Using the template cut the fan shape from a piece of tracing paper. Glue to one side of the 'embroidered' loop. Leave to dry.

9 Using a fine brush draw a simple flower shape onto the fan's paper surface.

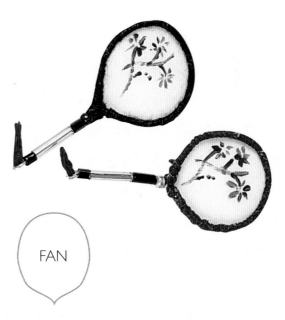

FAN

Materials
Thin cardboard
Decorative paper
Thin ribbon
PVA glue
Selection of black and white 'prints'

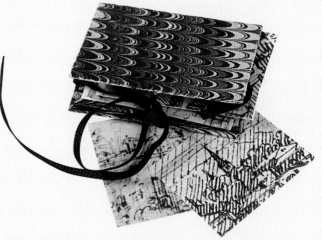

1 Cut a rectangle of thin card using the template. Carefully score the middle fold line.

2 Cut a rectangle of decorative paper just a little larger all around than the template.

3 Glue the paper to one side of the rectangle folding the excess to the inside.

4 Glue the side ribbons in place as indicated, which will cause the portfolio to assume a deep 'V' shape.

5 Glue the two tie ribbons in place.

6 Cut two pieces of decorative paper to fit each inner side of the portfolio. These will cover the folded edges and the ends of the ribbons.

7 Carefully glue these pieces of paper in place.

8 Fill the portfolio with a selection of suitable images and tie up.

Art portfolio

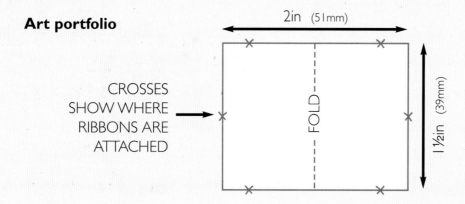

CROSSES SHOW WHERE RIBBONS ARE ATTACHED

2in (51mm)

FOLD

1½in (39mm)

Round Pictures

Materials
Pictures
Dome stickers (or acetate)
Thin card
Narrow gold braid
Narrow black ribbon
Black acrylic paint
PVA glue

1 Select part of a picture and position the dome sticker over it.

2 Cut around the sticker leaving a margin that is wide enough to stick the gold ribbon on.

3 Glue the picture onto a piece of thin card, then glue the gold ribbon carefully around the outside border.

4 If you wish, give the ribbon a wash of black paint to dull it down.

5 Tie a bow in a length of black ribbon and glue to the top of the picture trailing the ends down the back of the picture (glue to secure) and cutting to a point about 1in (25mm) below.

Document Box

Materials
Mountboard
Wood veneer
Strips of paper
Red ribbon or thread
Black felt-tip pen

1 Cut the pieces using the templates.

2 Glue together with the coloured side of the mountboard inwards. Colour the exposed edges of the mountboard using a black felt-tip pen.

3 Cover the exterior with thin wood veneer.

4 Roll up strips of paper (around a bamboo skewer to get the shape) to make documents and secure with red ribbon or thread. Place inside box.

Document box

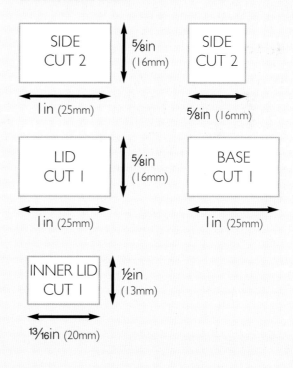

SIDE CUT 2 — $\frac{5}{8}$in (16mm) / 1in (25mm)

SIDE CUT 2 — $\frac{5}{8}$in (16mm)

LID CUT 1 — $\frac{5}{8}$in (16mm) / 1in (25mm)

BASE CUT 1 — 1in (25mm)

INNER LID CUT 1 — $\frac{1}{2}$in (13mm) / $\frac{13}{16}$in (20mm)

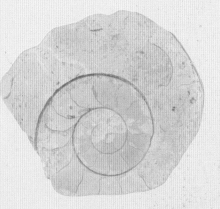

A model ship (here a gift shop item) can spark off a whole decorative scheme to add character to your dolls' house. Look for other nautical items (a picture of seascapes, a lifebouy, telescope or globe, to suggest that your gentleman has a sea-faring background.

Small archaeological finds, such as this fossil and tiny shells from beach-combing, make perfect natural additions to the gentleman's study.

This small vase from a gift shop fits neatly into the dolls' house as an umbrella stand. Likewise, this full size thimble makes a dolls' house sized wastepaper bin in the gentleman's study.

Afternoon

In the Drawing Room

When not out visiting or walking, the young lady of wealth keeps herself occupied as idleness is frowned upon. Time is spent in the withdrawing room (a room regarded as a feminine preserve) or in the parlour.

Many of the rooms in the Victorian house look cluttered, with every available surface given over to display, and the drawing room is no exception. Here, the top of the piano provides refuge for a bowl of nuts, a classical statue, a violin and a bust of Queen Victoria herself. The low table and the whatnot are also full of ornaments, books and odds and ends. To keep the lady occupied there is a sewing box on the chaise so that she can practise her embroidery skills.

Ornate Mirror

Materials
Mirror card
Mountboard
Self-adhesive braid
PVA glue
Black and gold acrylic paint
Varnish

Note: If you can't find self-adhesive braid use ordinary braid instead and glue it in position using PVA glue. You may find braid available in gold or black, but if not you can always paint it as has been done here.

1 Cut a piece of mirror card to comfortably fit the chimney breast.

2 Cut a piece of mountboard ¼in (6mm) larger all round than the mirror card.

3 Paint a ½in (13mm) border all around the edge of the mountboard with black or gold paint, plus the thin edge of the mountboard too. Leave to dry.

4 Glue the piece of mirror card to the mountboard.

5 Cut a piece of braid to fit around each side of the mirror card, overlapping it slightly. Mitre the corners neatly.

6 Dab on black acrylic paint carefully and pick out areas with gold when dry if wished.

7 Apply a coat of varnish to the braid when the paint has dried.

Silver Candlesticks

Materials
Strips of white paper, 1in (25mm) wide by about 5in (127mm) long
Wooden cocktail stick
Small amount of black crochet cotton
Glue stick
Tacky Glue
Four silver-coloured eyelets
One silver-coloured washer
Small piece of thin card

1 Roll the paper around the cocktail stick firmly then unwind. The paper will retain a curl.

2 Continue to roll the paper between your finger and thumbs several times until it rolls really tightly. Wetting your fingers slightly helps.

3 Lay a length of black crochet cotton at one end of the paper strip and roll the paper up tightly with the cotton in the middle. Use a glue stick to secure the roll. The finished roll of paper (the candle) should fit neatly inside the eyelet.

4 Rub a little Tacky Glue on the bottom half of the paper roll and push on four silver eyelets. Trim the black cotton off at the base, but leave a wick at the top.

5 Glue a washer to the bottom of the last eyelet, and a small circle of card to the bottom of this. Leave to dry.

6 Carefully add drops of Tacky Glue around the top of the candle, brushing it through the wick to stiffen it, and add drips down the length of the candle using the tip of the cocktail stick. Leave to dry.

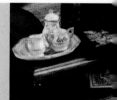

Another occupation for filling the hours is making use of shells collected on trips to the seaside. At home these are used to make pictures (as is dried seaweed) and decorate boxes. There is always embroidery to do, from monogrammed handkerchiefs to elaborate pictures, not to mention crochet, lacework and knitting.

Materials
Mountboard
Thin card
Red hand-made paper
Tacky Glue
Black felt-tip pen
Wood veneer
Tiny shells
Varnish
Thin ribbon

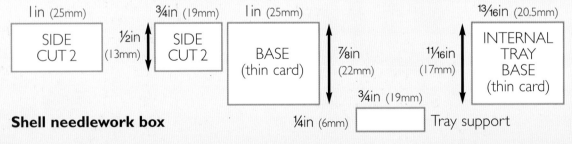

1 From the mountboard cut the box using the templates. Cut the base from thin card.

2 Glue the longer sides between the shorter ones. Glue to the base. Leave to dry.

3 Colour exposed edges of the top of the box with black felt-tip pen.

4 Cut two strips of ribbon to form hinges and stick against the back leaving a small amount that will be glued to the underneath of the lid.

5 Line the box with thin red paper.

6 Cover the long sides of the box with veneer. Do this by placing the box on a piece of veneer and scoring around it carefully with a scalpel. Cut across the grain first. Glue in place. Leave to dry. Repeat with the shorter sides.

7 Use fine sandpaper or a flexible sanding block and carefully sand each surface.

8 Place the box on a piece of thin card board and draw around it to get the size of the lid.

9 Cut out and cover with veneer. Leave to dry then sand as before.

10 Apply a thick layer of Tacky Glue over the whole lid, then arrange a group of shells on it in a pattern. Leave to dry.

11 Glue the ends of the ribbon hinges to the bottom of the lid, making sure that the lid will open and close neatly. Cover the inside of the lid with red paper to cover the ribbon ends.

Making the internal tray

1 Use an internal tray using ⅛in (3mm) strips of mountboard to form the sides, glued to a ¹¹⁄₁₆ x ¹³⁄₁₆in (17 x 20.5mm) thin card base.

2 Cover the tray with red paper, gluing on two ribbon handles to the inside before covering the bottom of the tray.

1in (25mm) · ¾in (19mm) · 1in (25mm) · ¹³⁄₁₆in (20.5mm)

| SIDE CUT 2 | ½in (13mm) | SIDE CUT 2 | BASE (thin card) | ⅞in (22mm) / ¾in (19mm) | 1¹⁄₁₆in (17mm) | INTERNAL TRAY BASE (thin card) |

Shell needlework box

¼in (6mm) · Tray support

Decoupage Tray

Materials
Mountboard
Tacky Glue
Small pictures of flowers
Black acrylic paint
Varnish

1 Cut out the pieces for the tray from mountboard, using a metal rule and sharp scalpel.

2 Carefully cut out the handle section using the scalpel.

3 Glue the sides on top of the base and leave to dry.

4 Paint the whole of the tray black.

5 When dry glue small pictures of flowers to the centre of the tray.

6 Varnish when the glue has completely dried.

Decoupage tray

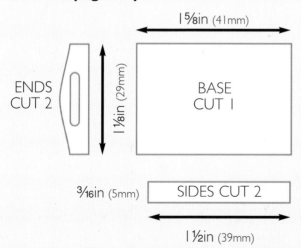

ENDS CUT 2

1⅝in (41mm)

1⅛in (29mm)

BASE CUT 1

³⁄₁₆in (5mm)

SIDES CUT 2

1½in (39mm)

Oval Firescreen

Materials
Two staircase spindles
Mountboard
Top of chess piece (castle/rook)
Rub-down transfers (rose design)
Black and gold acrylic paint
Black picot braid
Satin varnish

1 Cut the oval shape from the mountboard.

2 Carefully saw off the crenellated top of the chess piece. Drill a small hole in the centre of the removed piece.

3 Push a spindle into the hole of the chess piece, sanding it slightly if necessary.

4 Paint all the pieces black and leave to dry. Paint gold highlights where required.

5 Decorate one side of the mountboard oval with rub-down transfers.

6 Glue the oval to the top ⅝in (16mm) of the spindle that is mounted in the chess piece base.

7 Cut a section of the second spindle to be glued on top of the lower spindle at the back of the oval, to protrude ½in (13mm) above the oval.

8 Paint this additional spindle black and gold.

9 When the paint is dry varnish the whole piece, putting at least two layers on the screen face itself.

FIRE SCREEN CUT 1

Oval fire screen

For realism in your dolls' house avoid having copies of very famous paintings and instead find subjects that correspond to

the favourite themes of the time. These include landscapes and rustic scenes, domestic life conveying homely sentiments, children at play or animals.

Made from chess pieces from a redundant set and discs of thin wood sheeting, this whatnot is perfect to display an array of pieces of Victoriana.

The firescreen is an important cosmetic aid for this Victorian lady. It shields her complexion from the heat of the fire. Keeping a delicate pale skin is a sign of class, indicating that she doesn't have to work outside in the open air and be prey to the elements.

In the Kitchen

Afternoon tea is being prepared in the kitchen. This is eaten around four o'clock in the afternoon and is regarded as a light meal, filling the gap between luncheon and dinner. It generally includes bread and butter, biscuits, cake and tea.

Tea also needs to be prepared for serving at four o'clock up in the nursery. This usually consists of bread and butter and jam and cake. Sometimes the parents will join their children for nursery tea.

If high tea is required instead this is eaten a little later, between five and six in the evening. It is more of a meal with items such as pork and salmon being on the menu. There is also a selection of cakes and tarts, with teabreads and cheeses too. Tea, coffee and cocoa might also be on offer.

By the 1880s taking tea is quite a social event with the ladies wearing specific 'tea gowns' for the occasion. The events serve as a chance to exchange gossip and meet new acquaintances.

Tea Caddy

The housekeeper is in charge of blending the tea, which at the beginning of Queen Victoria's reign is blended at home. It isn't unknown for servants to sell on used tea leaves, which would be dried on hot plates and even dyed.

Materials

Mountboard (grey on one side)
Acrylic burnt umber, burnt sienna, brown and yellow ochre paints
Satin varnish
Tea leaves

1   Cut out the pieces from mountboard.

2   Glue the end and side pieces onto the base, with the grey colour facing inwards. Clamp while drying.

3   Glue the divider section together with the grey surfaces on the outside. Glue this in the middle of the box.

4   On a piece of paper paint a section of tortoiseshell using a mixture of brown and yellow ochre paint.

5   Cut pieces from the tortoiseshell to cover each side of the box, and another for the lid. You may find this easier by placing each box side in turn on top of the paper and cutting around it with a scalpel.

6   Glue the two small lid supports to the reverse of the lid.

7   Varnish all sides of the tea caddy.

8   Fill the compartments with glue and add real tea leaves.

Tea caddy

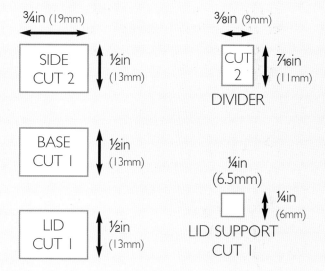

¾in (19mm)

SIDE
CUT 2   ½in (13mm)

BASE
CUT 1   ½in (13mm)

LID
CUT 1   ½in (13mm)

⅜in (9mm)

CUT 2   ⁷⁄₁₆in (11mm)

DIVIDER

¼in (6.5mm)

¼in (6mm)

LID SUPPORT
CUT 1

Scones

Materials

Caramel coloured craft foam
¼in (6mm) cutter with flower motif
Paper plate
Small amounts brown and cream acrylic paint
PVA glue

1   Cut out a dozen or so flower shapes from the craft foam to make the scones.

2   Glue the shapes to a paper plate.

3   Using a very fine paintbrush apply dots of brown and cream paint on to the top of each scone.

Afternoon tea is not just an opportunity to meet friends and exchange gossip; it is also a chance to show off not only the tea set, but also the quality of the tablecoth (preferably damask and lace-edged) and the table!

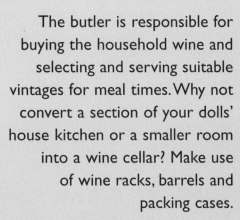

The butler is responsible for buying the household wine and selecting and serving suitable vintages for meal times. Why not convert a section of your dolls' house kitchen or a smaller room into a wine cellar? Make use of wine racks, barrels and packing cases.

The butler is in charge of the male servants in the house. His dress would be smart but would include a deliberate fashion faux pas, such as a coloured waistcoat, to distinguish him from gentleman guests. In larger households he will command his own suite of rooms including a bedroom, parlour, lockable plate room and work rooms for minor chores.

Early Evening

In the Master Bedroom

The mistress is dressing to meet the guests for a dinner party at home. Depending upon her social engagements up to six changes of outfit may be required in one day. The lady's maid helps with this task where wardrobe and cosmetic duties are vital. Knowledge of what is in fashion and what is not is a considerable advantage. French maids are seen as skilled in these regards and are often preferred to their English counterparts.

Silver Brushes

Materials
Two pieces of mountboard, each ⅝ x ¼in
(16 x 6mm)
Small piece of Velcro fastener
Silver acrylic paint
Sticky silver motifs (peelies)
Satin varnish

---

1 Gently curve the ends of the two
   pieces of mountboard. Begin by cutting
   a triangular section off each corner
   then, holding the mountboard between
   your finger and thumb, use a sanding
   block to smooth the curve.

2 Cut a piece of the Velcro fastener and
   stick to one of the mountboard pieces.
   Trim to the same shape as the
   mountboard. Repeat with the loop
   fastener for the other piece.

3 Paint the mountboard with silver acrylic
   paint and leave to dry.

4 Decorate the silver side with peelies,
   cutting the filigree pattern to fit if
   necessary, then varnish.

Silver Mirror

**The mirror is glued to the dressing-table
cloth making the construction easier.**

Materials
½in (13mm) diameter mirror circle
(from craft shops)
Fine (beading) wire
Small silver beads
1 small black bead
1 tube bead
Tacky Glue

---

1 Thread a number of small silver beads
   onto a length of wire.

2 Wrap the wire around the mirror to
   form a loop. Twist the wire to secure.

3 You can remove the excess wire at this
   point from one end to leave one piece.
   Bend this remaining length of wire at
   90 degrees to form the handle.

4 Onto this piece of wire thread one
   black then one silver bead, the tube
   bead, then the remaining silver bead.

5 Cut off the rest of the wire to leave a
   very small piece that can be bent into a
   loop.

6 Decide where you want to place the
   mirror on the cloth then glue it down.
   Add a little glue to the handle, place
   the wire loop over the mirror and glue
   the handle in position.

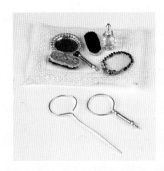

Dressing-table Cloth

The lace cloth is glued to a thin piece of card to make any items placed on it easier to glue on and to keep them secure.

Materials
Cotton fabric 1¾ x 1⅛in (44 x 28mm)
Thin card 1¾ x 1⅛in (44 x 28mm)
PVA glue
Fine lace

1 Glue the cotton fabric to the card and leave to dry. You may need to check that the card isn't warping. Curl it back with your fingers if necessary.

2 Cut the lace into four pieces to edge each side, mitring the ends. A fine antique lace works well for this project.

Perfume Bottle

You can use any combination of beads to make these simple items. Glue the bottles to the dressing tablecloth.

Materials
Two gold jump rings; one large, one small
Glass faceted bead
Back of earring stopper
Brass pin
Tacky Glue

1 Glue the large jump ring to the dressing-table cloth.

2 Glue the glass bead on top of the jump ring.

3 Glue the smaller jump ring on top of the glass bead, then glue the earring stopper on top.

4 Push a brass pin through the whole assembly through the holes.

Hat-pin Stand

Materials
Small piece of cork
Thin velvet-type material in crimson
Narrow red ribbon
Gold picot braid
Black paper
Tacky Glue
Dressmaking pins
Selection of beads

1 Slice a ³⁄₁₆in (5mm) section off the cork. Trim down from this to leave a ½in (13mm) diameter, circle.

2 Cut a circle of velvet-type material to cover the cork, and glue it over the cork, pulling it taut. It may take a while for the glue to dry, try to hold the material until it is firm.

3 Wrap a length of ribbon around the base, then a length of picot braid.

4 Cover the base of the circle in black paper.

5 To make the hat pins add a dollop of Tacky Glue near the head of a pin and thread on a selection of beads.

6 Using pliers trim the length of the pins slightly before pushing them carefully into the cork. Make sure that they don't push through the base paper.

Tiara

Materials
Fine beading wire
15 round beads
10 small tube beads

Note: Begin the tiara design in the middle and work outwards equally on either side.

1 Thread on a round bead with a tube bead either side. Twist the beading wire to contain these.

2 Thread on three round beads, then two tube beads on either side. Twist the tube beads so that they are contained.

3 Add on three round beads, two tube beads then one round bead at the end.

4 Trim the wire close to the final beads then wrap the end of the wire over and around the final bead to secure.

5 Gently bend the tiara into shape.

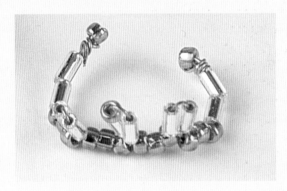

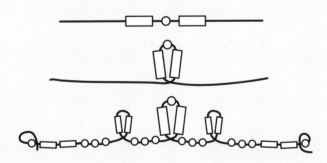

Shooting fancy fowl provided many feathers for the fashion industry – both for fans and on hats. This trend was responsible for the extinction of many species.

The mirrors on this wardrobe have been added and smudged with black paint to age them. Fill your dolls' house wardrobe with items and leave the door ajar to reveal just a glimpse of the contents. The imagination will supply the rest!

To add to that typical cluttered Victorian look make sure that bedroom chairs are draped with shawls and fripperies. Cover your chair in plastic food wrap then drape a wallpaper-paste soaked piece of lace (here a small doiley) over the back, arranging the folds to suit. Leave to dry then remove the plastic food wrap and re-set the lace.

In the Parlour

Before going in to dine the guests gather around the piano for some pleasant entertainment. Playing the piano is a popular accomplishment for a lady. One of the guests may suggest a song or even offer to sing.

Piano

A piano is easier to make than may appear – it is basically a rectangular box with a shelf along the front. You can make it firmer by cutting sheets of thick corrugated cardboard (or a polystyrene block) to fill the interior (or build the mountboard around a corrugated card block).

Materials
Mountboard
Two staircase spindles
Two wooden clothes pegs
Woodstrip, 1¹⁄₁₆ x ¼ x 4½in
(27 x 6 x 114mm)
¹⁄₁₆in (2mm) square woodstrip
Jumbo lolly stick (try craft shops)
Fancy moulding
PVA glue
Sticky gold motifs ('peelies')
Acrylic paint in shades of brown
Varnish
Two gold flat beads
Small amount of white paper
Black cotton

Making the piano body

1 Divide a wooden clothes peg in two, retaining the wire sections. Cut 1⁷⁄₈in (48mm) from the rounded end on both pieces, reserving the sloped ends. Sand the cut edges, and any rough surface on the pegs.

2 Drill a hole to take the end of the staircase spindle in the end of the clothes peg.

3 Cut the pieces of mountboard using the templates.

4 Glue the sides, back and front together.

5 Glue on the top piece keeping the assembly square.

6 Cut a piece of thin card for the base. Glue the pieces of clothes pegs in position as indicated.

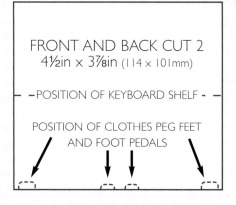

Piano (Diagrams at 50% of actual size)

FRONT AND BACK CUT 2
4½in x 3⁷⁄₈in (114 x 101mm)

– POSITION OF KEYBOARD SHELF – –

POSITION OF CLOTHES PEG FEET
AND FOOT PEDALS

SIDE CUT 2
1in x 3⁷⁄₈in (25mm x 101mm)

7 Take one of the sloped pieces of clothes peg and cut it in two to make the two foot pedals. Glue these in the middle of the base.

8 Carefully glue the base to the main body of the piano.

Adding the keyboard

1 Gently round the two front corners of the piece of woodstrip that holds the keyboard.

2 Glue the wood strip about 2in (51mm) up from the base of the piano.

3 Cut two pieces of peg to fit either side of the keyboard area and glue in place.

4 Stick the paper keyboard onto a piece of mountboard and glue into position.

Piano (Diagrams at 50% of actual size)

```
┌─────────────────────────────────┐
│        TOP  AND  BASE           │
│  1⅛in x 4½in   (28.5mm x 114mm) │
└─────────────────────────────────┘
```

Cut 1 from mountboard
Cut 1 from thin card

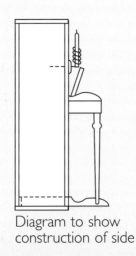

Diagram to show construction of side

5 Measure the distance between the keyboard and the footrest and cut the two spindles accordingly, making sure that there is a small amount to fit in the pre-drilled holes.

6 Glue the spindles between the feet and the keyboard shelf.

Finishing off

1 Cut a piece of jumbo lolly stick to fit over the keyboard, glue a length of ¹⁄₁₆in (3mm) square woodstrip along one long edge.

2 Trim the top of the piano with fancy moulding, leaving it a little proud of the piano top to form a lip.

3 Paint the assembly in shades of brown acrylic. Stick gold motifs on and add several coats of paint on top to dull down their colour.

4 Apply varnish when dry.

Adding the candles

1 To make one candle carefully cut the spring clip from one of the clothes pegs with a pair of pliers to provide the spiral shaft and one 'arm'.

2 Paint the metal with gold paint.

3 Make a candle to fit inside the metal shaft (see page 95). Make sure that the end of the paper roll is to the rear so not seen when viewing the piano.

4 Make a hole about 1in (25mm) down from the top of the piano close to the edge using a compass point.

5 Thread a flat gold bead onto the metal arm then insert the arm into the hole, gluing to keep it in place.

Music Stand

Materials
Wooden fan (or sheet of ¹⁄₁₆in (3mm) timber or wide lolly stick)
Small piece of fancy moulding
¹⁄₁₆in (3mm) square woodstrip
Brown and burnt sienna acrylic paint
Satin varnish
2 short pins

1 Use the end pieces of the wooden fan, which are thicker than the spokes. Cut the tops off the two ends to form the music sheet rest. If you don't have a fan, cut this shape as one whole piece from sheet timber, or use two ends of a lolly stick.

2 Cut a section from one end of a fan piece, or from sheet timber, to form the main pedestal of the music stand.

3 Cut two pieces of fancy moulding to go either side of the pedestal to act as 'feet'.

4 Cut pieces of the square woodstrip to go along the front of the music sheet rest, along the back of the rest at the top and bottom and, on the back, either side of the pedestal piece.

5 Glue the structure together and paint when dry with a mix of the two paint shades.

6 Varnish when dry.

7 Carefully drill two very tiny holes

through the bottom of the music rest. Insert a pin through each and carefully bend using pliers. Snip off the pointed end to leave about ⅛in (6mm) proud. Apply a little glue over the pin to hold it upright.

Music stand

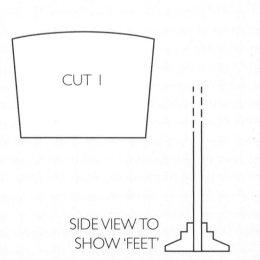

CUT 1

SIDE VIEW TO SHOW 'FEET'

CUT 1

A Serenade

Schubert

English words by
J Trowbeck

The Victorians have a whole language of flowers; selecting the right colour of rose for example can convey love, friendship or regret. The suitor must be sure to get it right.

The piano has become a status symbol for the class conscious Victorians. Playing the instrument is considered genteel and women aspired to become accomplished in the task. For the leisured classes playing the piano whiles away the hours and, more importantly, entertains at social gatherings.

The rules governing mourning are strict. For women mourning involves the wearing of black for several months (depending on the closeness of the relationship with the deceased). This can then be followed by grey and purple. Mourning outfits also extend to the household servants.

In the Dining Room

The dining room is 'masculine' in terms of decor. Red or green damask on the walls is a popular choice, with the colours chosen to contrast with the crisp linen tablecloth and silver accessories.

The meal is presided over by the butler, supervising the footmen and making sure that everything is served correctly and that guests' needs are attended to. The butler is responsible for making sure that the wine cellar is suitably stocked, and appropriate wines served. The family's silver utensils are also under his charge.

Each place is set with an intricately folded napkin, cutlery (for all courses) and glasses (set to the right of the diner) for sherry, claret and champagne. As the nineteenth century reached its closing years the table would also feature several towering floral displays, occasionally incorporating water features. The meal may consist of up to nine courses; soup, fish, an entrée, a meat course, poultry, sweets, cheeses, ices and finally fruit. The numerous courses enable diners to make a choice to suit their tastes. Diners could refuse a dish, but not ask for a second helping of one.

Dinner Gong

Materials

2 square-shaped staircase spindles
¼in (6mm) wooden beading for glass windows
3 wooden cocktail sticks
4 jump rings
Small length of fine chain
Aluminium drinks can
Acrylic paint in tin, old gold, burnt umber and burnt sienna
Satin varnish
Small 'eye' screw
Tacky Glue
A mini drill and strong scissors or tin snips are also useful for this project

---

1   Cut the two staircase spindles to a length of 2¾in (70mm), leaving a longer square section at the bottom of the spindle.

2   Select a drill bit with the same diameter as the cocktail sticks. Drill two holes in each spindle, the lower one being ½in (13mm) from the bottom.

3   Cut four sections from the window beading, each measuring the same width as the staircase spindle.

4   Glue a piece of the beading either side of each spindle to form a wider base.

5   Cut two of the cocktail sticks into 1¾in (44mm) lengths. Insert these into the drilled holes to form the two cross-members of the gong stand.

6   Paint the assembly (and the third cocktail stick) in a mixture of the burnt umber and burnt sienna acrylic paint. Leave to dry.

7   Slightly crush the drinks can and cut the fold with strong scissors or tin snips. Cut through to release the base.

8   Use a compass and mark a 1¼in (32mm) circle on the base to form the gong. Cut this out and gently file the edges with a fine sanding block.

9   Drill two holes to the top edges of the tin circle.

10 Paint the circle with coat of tin (or dark grey) coloured paint. When this has dried use a piece of sponge to dab on an old gold colour. Leave to dry before painting the other side of the gong.

11 Using a small pair of pliers to prise the jump ring apart. Attach each jump ring to the ends of two lengths of fine chain.

12 Attach the jump rings to the gong, and to the top cross-member.

13 Make a drumstick by cutting a length of the remaining painted cocktail stick. Glue a small wooden bead to the end.

14 Use a small 'eye' to make a holder for the drumstick. Carefully drill a hole to make the insertion easier. Alternatively make a loop of thread and glue to the end of the drumstick and hang round one of the spindles.

Materials

Wooden dish and cup (children's dolls' house accessories)
Bamboo skewer
Silver acrylic paint
Sticky filigree ('peelies') (optional)
Satin varnish
Ivy trails (laser-cut for scrapbooking – see step 6)
Silk roses on wire
Selection of foliage material
Selection of flowers

Note: Children's dolls' house accessories are often rather chunky but they are inexpensive. This arrangement makes use of a wooden bowl and cup.

1. Drill a hole in the centre of the bowl and the cup base that is wide enough to take the bamboo skewer. It needs to be a tight fit.

2. Cut a 2in (51mm) length from the skewer and insert into the dish at the bottom with the cup at the top.

3. Paint the assembly with silver paint and leave to dry.

4. If you wish decorate the dish and stem with stick on 'peelies' to give the appearance of a decorative pattern.

5. Varnish the assembly and leave to dry.

6. Glue ivy trails (those used here are from a set used for modern scrapbooking, but you can buy brass ivy trails from dolls' house suppliers) so that they tumble out of the top cup. If your ivy leaves are a uniform colour, gently sponge on a different green paint to vary the shade and make them look more natural.

7. Gather a number of silk roses, bind together and cut the wires short so that they fit into the cup.

8. In-fill around the roses with foliage material, remembering to trail some over the edge of the cup. Put a dollop of glue into the cup and carefully push this assembly into place.

9. Glue a mixture of foliage and flowers into the bottom dish.

Note: Instead of using flowers you may like to fill the bottom dish with a selection of fruit – make your own from Fimo, or buy ready-made fruit. Try a selection of grapes and apricots for a colour contrast.

Wine Cooler

This wine cooler (cellarette) is designed to retain six plastic dolls' house wine bottles. You can make a cooler to fit other bottles by using the same method and adjusting your measurements accordingly.

Materials
Scraps of mount board or 1/16in (3mm) thick card
Black felt-tip pen or black paint
Wood veneer
Tacky Glue
Varnish
2 drawer handles
4 map pins

1 Using the templates, cut the four sides, base and top from the mount board or card and glue them onto the base with the shorter sides fitting between the long ones. Leave to dry.

2 Colour the top edges of mount board with black felt-tip pen or paint.

3 Place one of the short sides of the box on a strip of wood veneer and cut around using a craft knife or scalpel. Glue the wood veneer onto the short side.

4 Repeat step 3 with the other short side, then repeat for the two remaining sides. Make sure that the wood grain runs in the same direction. Leave to dry.

5 Place the box on a piece of mount board or card and trace around to make a piece for the lid. Colour the edges of the mountboard black.

6 Glue a piece of wood veneer onto the lid of the wine cooler.

7 Create two more pieces of mount board and veneer to make a 'step'-shaped lid (see picture).

8 Glue a slightly smaller piece of mount board to fit underneath the lid to keep it in place.

9 Varnish, and when dry glue a handle to each side of the wine cooler.

10 Push a map pin into the bottom of the base, then withdraw the pin. Cut each pin shorter then apply a little glue and insert into the previously made hole.

Wine cooler

BASE CUT 1 1⅛in × 1⅜in (29 × 35mm)	SIDES CUT 2 1½in × 1⅜in (38mm × 35mm)

SIDES CUT 2 1½in × 1in (38mm × 25mm)

By the late Victorian times ornate floral displays are essential to grace the dining room table. If space permits these might include some form of water feature too. The careful placing of ice cubes on a top tier can precipitate a waterfall during the course of the evening as the ice melts and cascades below.

The butler will have selected the perfect vintages for the evening's courses. In the dining room a wine cooler keeps the bottles close to hand and ready to serve. Being on display they are inevitably fine looking pieces.

When guests are called to the dining room by the striking of the gong, a set of precedence determines in what order they take their places. First, the master of the house leads in his wife, and they choose who comes next.

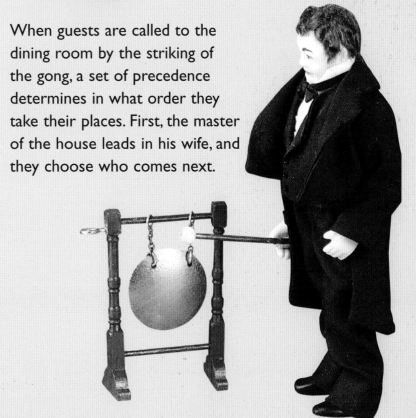

Night-Time

In the Dining Room

After the meal the hostess leads the ladies into the drawing room for coffee while the men remain in the dining room to enjoy some port and cigars. The nature of the conversation is no doubt a little more bawdy without female companions present.

The smoking jacket is a popular male garment in Victorian times, designed specifically for the purposes of smoking tobacco. Considerate men wear a smoking jacket so that when they return to the ladies they don't take the smell of tobacco with them on their usual clothing and thus offend delicate nostrils. Smoking is very much a masculine activity, with cigars and pipes the preserve of the upper-class gentleman. Cigarettes are associated with the working-class male, generally perceived to be unable to appreciate the finer qualities that the cigar contained.

Cigar Box

Materials
Thin white card
Gumstrip sealing tape
Black or brown felt-tip pen
Brown and yellow Fimo (to mix)
Paper

1 Cut the box shape according to the template.

2 Score carefully along the indicated lines.

3 Cover the inside with gumstrip sealing tape. The easiest way to do this is to wet an area of tape and place the card shape face-down on top. When it is dry, cut around the card with a scalpel.

4 Lightly score the fold marks again and fold up the box with the taped side on the inside.

5 Carefully colour any exposed (cut) edges of the card with a black or brown felt-tip pen.

6 Cut a strip of sealing tape to fit around the edges of the box, plus a little extra to fold beneath. Cut at the corner the section that will end up underneath. This will hold the box sides in position.

7 Cover the lid and base with gumstrip sealing tape and leave to dry.

8 Make a number of cigars from Fimo to fit inside the box. Roll pale brown Fimo into sausage shapes and bake according to manufacturer's instructions.

9 When the cigars are cold add a tiny paper band across the middle. Glue into the box.

10 Decorate the box as wished.

Cigar box

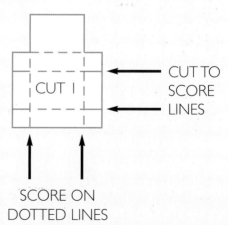

CUT 1

CUT TO SCORE LINES

SCORE ON DOTTED LINES

A decanter of whisky or port on the side table is essential in the Victorian dining room.

For a touch of realism leave the table partly set to suggest what has gone before. This makes your dolls' house look more like a real house and less like a show home.

A gentleman's wardrobe is looked after by his valet. Dressing male dolls tends to involve more somber colours than for the ladies. Make the most of coloured waistcoats or army uniforms.

In the Kitchen

Meanwhile, in the kitchen, the aftermath of the family's evening meal is being dealt with. The mounds of crockery and cutlery are being scraped of the remains of food before being washed, dried and put away. All this has to be done before the servants can retire to bed.

Cutlery Tray

Materials
Tiny pieces of a wine cork
Miniature newspaper
Miniature cutlery
Mountboard
Thin and thick card
Green felt
Brown acrylic paint
Varnish

---

1 Cut out the sides of the cutlery tray, using the templates.

2 Glue the shorter sides between the long ones.

3 Cut the base from thick card. Glue the sides to the base. Leave to dry.

4 Paint the exterior of the box in brown. Varnish and leave to dry.

5 Cut two dividers from thick card.

6 Line the base and sides of the cutlery tray with green felt, gluing it in place.

7 Glue green felt over the dividers, and with a little glue on their ends and base glue them in position.

Pieces of cork would have been pushed between the prongs of forks to remove any stubborn particles of food. Spread out sheets of miniature newspaper across the dining table. Lay out a number of forks and beside these glue tiny pieces of cork. After washing and before being placed back in the tray the cutlery may have been buffed up with polish, so make sure that there is a cloth handy.

Cutlery tray

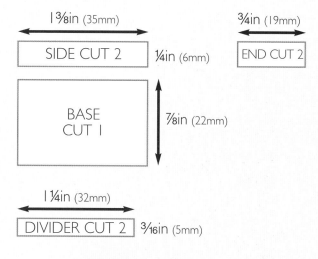

1⅜in (35mm) — SIDE CUT 2 — ¼in (6mm)

¾in (19mm) — END CUT 2

BASE CUT 1 — ⅞in (22mm)

1¼in (32mm) — DIVIDER CUT 2 — ³⁄₁₆in (5mm)

Plate Crate

Larger houses would have had a specific room to store their china dinner services and glassware.

Expensive dinner services would have been stored in chests with removable trays, lined with green baize, containing the various pieces. This example doesn't actually have a removable tray – but looks as though it does!

Materials
Mountboard
PVA glue
Tacky Glue
Gumstrip sealing tape
Dark green felt
Patterned paper
Paper plates
Polystyrene
Narrow ribbon
Black cotton tape
Wood veneer
Black paint
Varnish

1   From the mountboard cut the pieces for the plate crate using the templates. Use a scalpel and a metal ruler and cut on a cutting mat keeping the blade straight.

2   Glue the shorter sides between the longer ones by running a thin beading of glue along the cut edges. Then glue to the base. Reinforce all the joins with lengths of gumstrip sealing tape.

3   Make the box lid in the same fashion. Leave to dry.

4   Cover the inside edges of the lid, and the top ¾in (19mm) of the box interior with patterned paper.

5   Cut a piece of green felt to fit the inside of the box lid and glue into place.

6   Cut pieces of polystyrene to fill up the box finishing approximately ½in (13mm) below the top of the box.

7   Cut two lengths of ribbon to form handles and glue these on the interior of the two sides.

Plate crate

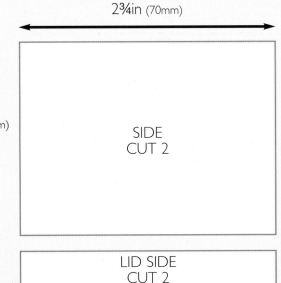

2⅛in (54mm)

SIDE
CUT 2

2in (50mm)

LID SIDE
CUT 2

⅜in (10mm)

2¾in (70mm)

SIDE
CUT 2

LID SIDE
CUT 2

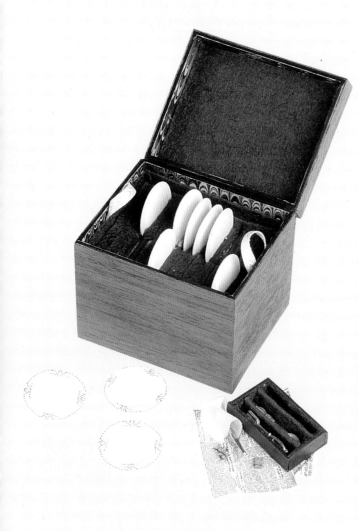

8 Glue a border of green felt to the interior of the box and to the top of the polystyrene. Leave to dry.

9 Using a sharp scalpel slice a number of slots into the polystyrene for the plates – the number is up to you. Here, there are two dozen.

10 Decorate the paper plates if you wish then push them carefully into position, leaving about two-thirds of each plate exposed.

11 Cut a length of cotton tape to form a hinge and, with the box lid sitting on top of the main section, glue the tape across the join. Leave to dry.

To veneer the box

1 Begin with one of the sides and the lid closed, place the box side down on a piece of veneer, ensuring the grain is running widthways.

2 Carefully draw the scalpel blade around the box and lid to cut it through.

3 Lift the box off the veneer, mark the lid piece on the veneer and slice that piece through.

4 Use Tacky Glue to glue the veneer to the side and lid side of the box.

5 Repeat for the second side. Then the front, then the back of the box. Finally mark out the lid. Glue and clamp as necessary while the glue dries. The base of the box is left as mountboard and should be painted black.

6 Carefully sand each surface with fine sandpaper and gently round the edges before varnishing.

2¾in (70mm)

2¼in (57mm)

BASE CUT 1
LID CUT 1

The fine dinner service is stored in a purpose-made box. Where such storage isn't available much use is made of china and glass cupboards lining the many corridors that run between the various servants' rooms.

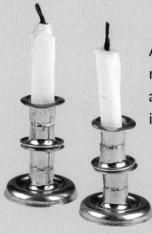

After a meal the remains of any food is scraped off the cutlery using pieces of cork. The cutlery is then washed, carefully! Implements made from stainless steel with ivory or bone handles need extra care. Not surprisingly special machines have been invented to make this task easier. They have emery boards and brushes are included in the mechanism to clean and sharpen.

Among his many duties it is also the responsibility of the butler to look after the candlesticks and any lamps in use (although he may pass this task on to a footman).
This involves cleaning, filling and delivering the lamps as required around the house.

In the Master Bedroom

With the guests departed, the master and mistress finally retire to bed.

The servants prepare the bedroom for the master and mistress of the house, laying out the night clothes and preparing a bath of hot water. Finally the servants can take themselves off to

their attic rooms to rest before their work begins early the following day.

Although the hours are long, if the family is pleasant at least the work is indoors rather than in the fields or factories. A good servant would hope to move through the ranks over the years to achieve status and more pay.

Bootjack

A bootjack helps a gentleman remove his boots. Left outside the bedroom overnight it would be the footman's job to clean the boots and return them the next day for his master's use.

Materials

Mountboard
Tacky Glue
Acrylic burnt umber and burnt
sienna paints
2 wooden cocktail sticks
2 square staircase spindles
Varnish

1 Mark out the footplate shape (see template) on mountboard.

2 Cut out the middle section of the footplate first, before cutting out the outline.

3 Using a scalpel carefully pare away at the square edges of the spindles to make them slightly more ornate.

4 Tape the spindles together and drill two holes (the diameter of the cocktail stick), one ³⁄₁₆in (5mm) from the top of the spindle, and the second ¾in (19mm) from the top.

5 Carefully push one cocktail stick through the lower hole to a width of ½in (13mm) or less. The footplate needs to be held snuggly between the two spindles, so adjust as necessary. Trim the cocktail stick flush at either side.

6 Repeat with the second cocktail stick to form the top brace. Leave a section protruding on each side to form handles.

7 Paint the structure with acrylic paint and varnish when dry.

8 Carefully glue the footplate between the bottom ledge of the spindles.

Bootjack

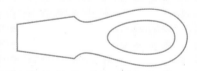

If you have a large Victorian dolls' house you might wish to have a family chapel in one of the smaller rooms, or divide off a section of one of the larger rooms to create one. Make use of stained glass windows and pew seating and install the family Bible.

Materials

Mountboard
Shades of brown acrylic paint
Satin varnish
PVA glue
Black felt
Short length of embroidered ribbon
Fray Check

1 Cut out two outer sides and two inner sides from mountboard. Stack the pieces on top of each other to make sure that they are identical before cutting the inner sides to shape.

2 Glue the inner sides to the outer ones making sure that you end up with a matched pair, not two identical sides. Hold until the glue begins to take.

3 Cut out the shelf and back support. Glue the shelf into position and hold until the glue begins to take. Then glue the back support into position.

4 Cut and glue the top book rest into position, adding a book support cut from a narrow strip of mountboard to the front edge.

5 Glue the kneeler into position. Paint the assembly brown and when dry, apply a coat of varnish.

6 Cut two pieces of black felt to match the kneeler. Glue these together, then glue in position on the kneeler.

7 Cut a length of embroidered ribbon to length, aligning any design so that it is central to the prie-dieu. Or embroider a short length for the kneeler to add your own personal touch.

8 Fray Check the ends of the ribbon. Glue on top of the black felt, pushing firmly along the front and back length. (The prie-dieu is pictured on page 35.)

Prie-dieu

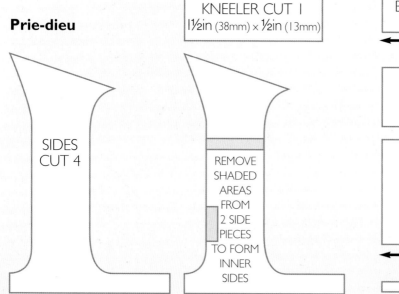

KNEELER CUT 1
1½in (38mm) × ½in (13mm)

SIDES CUT 4

REMOVE SHADED AREAS FROM 2 SIDE PIECES TO FORM INNER SIDES

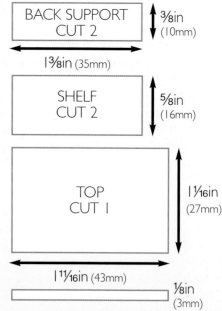

BACK SUPPORT CUT 2
⅜in (10mm)
1⅜in (35mm)

SHELF CUT 2
⅝in (16mm)

TOP CUT 1
1¹⁄₁₆in (27mm)
1¹¹⁄₁₆in (43mm)
⅛in (3mm)

Slipper Bath

Before bathrooms became commonplace, ceramic slipper baths are placed in bedrooms to enable a body wash. The maid brings up the hot water from the range in the kitchen, and empties the water after the ablutions have taken place.

Materials
Thin card
Russet-coloured felt
PVA glue
Wallpaper paste
Cream and white acrylic paint
Satin varnish

1 Cut out the side piece and base pieces from thin card.

2 Score and snip the marked section to enable the side to bend and form a 'ring' shape. Glue and clamp the 'ring'.

3 Apply glue to the tabs and glue a base 'inside' the bath and to the underneath, thus enclosing the tabs. Press firmly and hold until the glue takes. Leave to dry.

4 Paint the inside of the bath in a mixture of cream and white acrylic paint. Aim for a variation in surface colour to suggest wear. You can also apply a tiny amount of brown acrylic around the base and on the sides to suggest dirt, but blend it into the cream so that it is only barely perceptible. Leave to dry.

5 Carefully apply one or two coats of varnish to the inside of the bath.

6 Cover the outside of the bath with the felt, using the templates. Liberally cover the felt with two coats of wallpaper paste, allowing each to dry thoroughly. Apply three thick coats of PVA glue, allowing each coat to dry thoroughly.

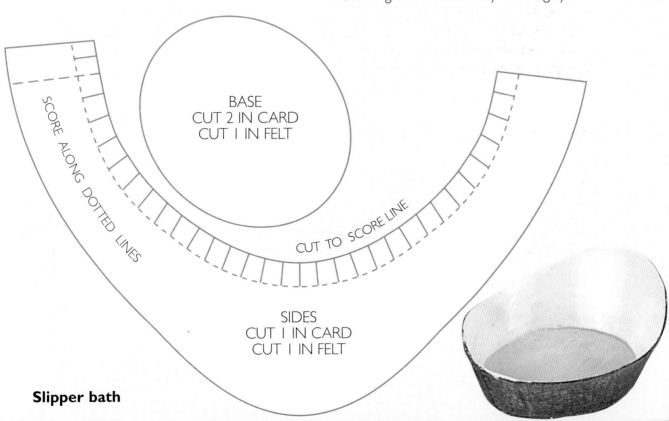

SCORE ALONG DOTTED LINES

BASE
CUT 2 IN CARD
CUT 1 IN FELT

CUT TO SCORE LINE

SIDES
CUT 1 IN CARD
CUT 1 IN FELT

Slipper bath

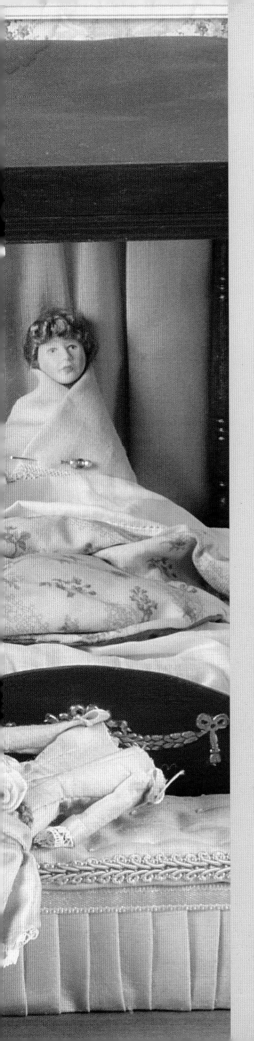

Domestic scenes are suitable for rooms where the ladies of the household might spend their time.

A family Bible is essential. Miniature versions are available through specialist suppliers.

Before the sewing machine was invented in 1851, dressmaking was a laborious task. With the advent of mechanical sewing and paper patterns women could soon update their wardrobes, although this often took the form of renovating or updating existing dresses rather than starting from scratch.

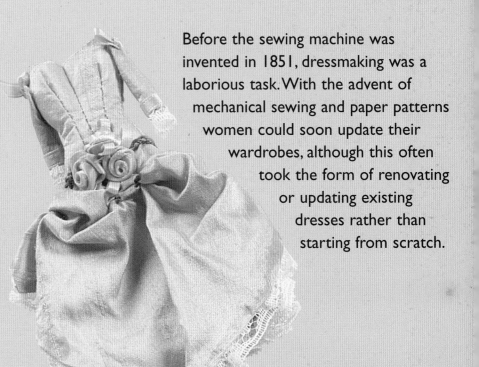

Index

Bibliography

Decorate a Dolls' House by Michal Morse, published by B T Batsford,
ISBN 0 7134 8288 5

The Period House, Style, Detail and Decoration 1774 – 1914 by Richard Russell Lawrence and Teresa Chris, published by Weidenfeld & Nicolson,
ISBN 0 297 83294 8

Suburban Style, The British Home 1840 – 1960 by Helena Barrett and John Phillips, published by Little, Brown & Co,
ISBN 0 316 90644 1

The Victorian Household Album by Elizabeth Drury and Philippa Lewis, published by Collins & Brown Ltd
ISBN 1 85585 221 7

Eating with the Victorians by C. Anne Wilson, ISBN 0750935510

The Party That Lasted 100 Days by Hilary and Mary Evans, published by Macdonald and Jane's Publishers
ISBN 0 356 083663 2

Victorian Painting by Julian Treuherz, published by Thames & Hudson,
ISBN 0 500 20263 X

Victorian House Style by Linda Osband, published by David & Charles,
ISBN 0 7153 9841 5

Care of Clothes by Jane Ashelford, published by The National Trust (Enterprises) Ltd, ISBN 0 7078 0223 7

About the Author

Christiane Berridge is the Editor of The Dolls' House Magazine and a passionate collector of dolls' houses and miniatures. She enjoys making items for her own dolls' houses and the projects contained in this book stem from her love of creativity. When not working or making miniatures you can find Christiane in the local theatre, where she is often engaged making the props required for various musicals and operas. Another evening activity is modern jive, which helps to counterbalance all those hours spent sitting at her worktable. Family activities takes up what little time there is left!

This is Christiane Berridge's second book, her first Making Miniatures, Projects for the 1:12 scale Dolls' House is also published by GMC.

With thanks to
The Dolls House Emporium for supplying various materials.
Miniature doll maker, Sue Harrington of 36 Nunney Road, Frome, Somerset, BA11 4LA (tel: 01373 464658) for kindly lending her porcelain dolls.
My Editor, Clare Miller, for all her work making sure that the production of this book actually happened.
Paul Berridge, for keeping our children occupied allowing me to make miniatures in peace.

For a complete catalogue or to place an order, contact:
GMC Publications, Castle Place, 166 High Street, Lewes, East Sussex, BN7 1XU, UK
Tel: 01273 488005   Fax: 01273 402866   Website: www.thegmcgroup.com
Orders by credit card are accepted